P9-CSC-532

# MONSTER

*Adventures in American Machismo*

# Monster

## ADVENTURES IN AMERICAN MACHISMO

Brian Bouldrey

COUNCIL OAK BOOKS
*San Francisco / Tulsa*

For Miriam Wolf,
friend, muse, confidante, editor

Council Oak Books, LLC
1290 Chestnut Street, Ste. 2, San Francisco, CA 94109
1350 E. 15th Street, Tulsa, OK 74120
MONSTER: *Adventures in American Machismo.*
Copyright © 2001 by Brian Bouldrey. All rights reserved.

Book design by Melanie Haage
Jacket design by Jason May

Grateful acknowledgment is made for permission to quote from
THE BIG ROCK CANDY MOUNTAIN by Wallace Stegner.
Copyright © 1938, 1940, 1942, 1943 by Wallace Stegner.
Used by permission of Doubleday, a division of Random House, Inc.

LIBRARY OF CONGRESS CATALOGING-IN-PUBLICATION DATA

Bouldrey, Brian.
Monster : adventures in American machismo /
Brian Bouldrey.— 1st ed.
p. cm.
ISBN 1-57178-106-4
1. Bouldrey, Brian. 2. Gay men—United States—
Biography.  3. Machismo—United States. 4. Men—
United States—Social life and customs.  I. Title.
HQ75.8.B657 A3 2001                    305.31'0973—dc21
2001032386

First edition / First printing.
Printed in Canada.
01  02  03  04  05  06  07   5  4  3  2  1

*"I'm daffy about flax anyway," Jud said. "Something about it makes me feel good. It's so slick and silky to feel." He ran his hand into the mouth of a sack and wriggled his fingers.*

*"We never grew it at home," Elsa said.*

*"Feel."*

*She pushed her hand into the brown flaky seeds. They slipped smoothly up her wrist, cool and dry, millions of polished, purple-brown, miniature guitar picks. She moved her hand and the flax swirled like heavy smooth water against her skin.*

*"That's nice," she said.*

*"It's something to see in flower, too," Jud said. "Acres of bluebells."*

*Her quick look acknowledged something sensitive, almost feminine, in the expression of his face as he caressed the flax with his fingers. "It's like everything else that's lovely," Jud said. "Dangerous. Boy was drowned in a flax bin here a year ago. Fell in and it sucked him down before anybody could get to him. We had to empty the whole bin to get him. Nice boy, too. That's the kind things always happen to. A mean, tough kid, now, he'd never know enough to appreciate the feel of flax, and he'd never get caught in it."*

**—Wallace Stegner,**
THE BIG ROCK CANDY MOUNTAIN

# CONTENTS

# 1

# SITTING STILL

ONE THING NOT VERY MANY PEOPLE KNOW ABOUT ME is that I once killed a bear. Actually, that's not true. A lot of people know this about me. It's a story I trot out under the influence, or even out from under the influence, a story told with a tortured mix of shame and pride; the situation involved Campfire Girls in the woods, and me protecting them with an AK-47. The bear attacked us. I had to shoot. All the children lived.

It has been more than fifteen years since I killed the bear, and basically, fifteen years since I held a gun in my hands. Guns don't interest me the way I guess they're supposed to, though I think it's fascinating how anything with the power to kill looks laughably, unsubtly, like a penis: rifles, swords, arrows, the Batmobile, syringes, the candlestick Colonel Mustard used in the conservatory. They are not "phallic symbols," they're *dick replacements*. Maybe Andrea Dworkin was right, and any penetration is an act of male aggression. That this is actually natural—that our survival depends on these things—is what should deeply trouble Dworkin. I'm troubled.

I am the oldest of three brothers. The next one, three years younger, the middle of the sibling sandwich, is Chris.

He and I fought so ferociously as kids that if we had had candlesticks or swords or Batmobiles at our disposal, we would have died before Chris was old enough to join the Marines, become a bodybuilder and prison guard, and pursue a life of endless hunting and fishing, which is what he did, or before I was old enough to kill a bear, which is what I did.

I was barely twenty when I killed the bear. It was while I worked in the Alaskan bush for a program through Campfire Incorporated (previously Campfire Girls, but fully coeducational by the time I tromped into the Yukon interior). After training, Campfire divided up a staff of twenty into twos and threes, and of all the luck, I was sent out into Athabaskan villages with Idamay, a patient, kayaking, British Columbian lesbian. She held me together body and soul. She played Strip Uno with me on our days off. She taught me how to make an entire meal out of muskrat and smoked salmon. And most important, she showed me how to use certain leaves to stanch the bleeding when my chest, numb as the rest of my body when teaching basic swimming skills to Native American kids in the glacier-fed Yukon River, became spangled with red dots after a curious smooth-skinned Athabaskan boy grabbed at my chest hair and pulled out a handful, the painful damage apparent only after I'd climbed out of the water and warmed up a little.

We'd been sent in, Idamay and I, to bring Good American Things to a people living at a subsistence level through fishing salmon and hunting various beasts. Water safety, physical fitness, nutrition (a jar of peanut butter and pilot bread), some arts and crafts (Popsicle sticks and glue)—we were a road-show summer camp. But when we blithely decided to take about twenty children, from ages four to fourteen, on a nature hike, a rough but realistic parent explained that no kid of his was going to go into the woods outside the village without the protection of a gun. He pulled out one of his own, a Vietnam vintage AK-47, which lay in my little homo hands like a bazooka.

Idamay looked at me. "Do you know how to use one of those?"

Funny, I did. I'd had enough of a boy's love for destructive power to get a First Class Marksmanship pin in Boy Scouts, spending my days firing rounds into paper targets purchased with pocket money earmarked by Mom for candy bars at the trading post of Camp Teetonkah. I turned to Idamay, shoved a clip full of ammunition into this monstrosity, aimed at a tree, and squeezed the trigger, neither flinching at the kickback when it burned my ear and bruised my shoulder, nor at the way I basically tore all the bark off a harmless spindly birch. I put the gun to my side, strode to Idamay, all plaid and boots, and minced, "You know, there's a *fabulous* sale at Macy's, we really have to go!" And later, on the trail, I shot the gun again, and the bear, like the bark of the birch, was no match.

After fifteen years, I flew home to Michigan to go hunting for a second time with my brother Chris, now an ex-Marine, a giant bodybuilding sports guy who turned his basement into a Guy Room, replete with rows of deer racks, gun racks, weight racks, and the framed picture of dogs playing poker, one of a set of six that were my grandfather's in *his* Guy Room, now split among his grandchildren the way Lear's land was, and causing as much trouble. But that is neither here nor there, and I don't bring it up here, now, when both Chris and I have guns in our hands.

Actually Chris is the kind of hunter you want all hunters to be like. He greatly prefers the tracking, the hunt of the hunt, and he mostly uses bows and arrows. Not only that, he uses bows and arrows he made himself, and the Guy Room also contains his workbench for the manufacture of these weapons.

Once he's cut the shafts of the arrows and just before they're fletched and a head is attached, he puts his six-year-old artistic daughter, Jaime, to work painting them. While the shaft spins round and round on a little lathe, this remarkably self-possessed blonde girl plans out complex bands and patterns of her favorite girly colors: bubble-gum pink, baby blue, good-as gold, shook-foil silver—the colors of nail polish, lip gloss, Barbie clothes—oddly perfect for use in the woods, where they're easily spotted on the mossy floor if they miss their target. It can't be lost on Chris, though, that he trails through the forest primeval with a quiver full of sissy arrows.

November is open gun season in Michigan. It's also Thanksgiving weekend, so competition is stiff. We're going out with guns, not arrows. Just as well, as I'd probably take the skin clean off my inner arm when letting go the bowstring; I can see it in my mind wrapped neatly round and round like a grizzly retractable window blind.

We're after deer, of course, and on the way from the airport in Detroit, we nearly hit a herd crossing the road from one new housing development to another, subdivisions that were once open woodland. That habitat does double-duty now. "Look at those gray herons," I remarked on an afternoon drive through a new neighborhood. "We never had gray herons flocking in our yard when I was a kid."

"Yes," my mother says, "they just started coming here a few years ago. Aren't they pretty?"

Later she shoos a deer out of her garden, and Uncle Jimmy is late for Thanksgiving dinner because he was out walking the dog and spotted a buck, ran into the house to grab his gun, and bagged it right there, and hung it from the rafters in his garage. He had to leave before the pumpkin pie, for the thing had to be dressed properly.

Autumn visits to my family usually involve a carcass of some sort, startling me when I enter the shed and think we've received a warning from the mob. No matter whether it's a buck or a doe, deer are doe-eyed, and they gaze at you like, well, a deer caught in the headlights. They are everywhere in Michigan, practically domesticated. People put salt licks in their yards, or crappy pasteboard cutouts of deer next to the plaster gnomes.

Hunting and fishing provide the cornerstone of my family's history. After Thanksgiving dinner, we sit around and talk first about Uncle Jimmy and how he fell in the water twice while fishing, how he tried to enter the annual Carp Carnival with a carp he'd speared four months too early and stuck in the freezer in the basement. Then all the stories come out, like the one about the Easter we were up north and a run of delicious speckled bass came up my grandmother's dead-end channel and the whole extended family dropped everything just to pull fish out of the lake. Then there was the year they limited one deer to every hunter, and my brother talked every woman in the family into registering as a hunter so he could use her allotted deer quota. Imagine my mother in a hunting coat, camouflage scarf, and boots, applying for her license at the bait shop down the road. Very convincing, in her Ray-Bans.

That law is gone now. Killing deer in Michigan is like shooting fish in a barrel. Which is not much fun for my brother. He hands me camouflage pants, a coat, and an orange cap. Big, long, lace-up boots. "It's no challenge to go out and shoot at whatever," he explains to me. "Which is why some of my hunting buddies get pissed off at me. I only get one or two big bucks a year. Those guys say I'm too picky, so I've been doing more and more of my hunting alone." Which may, after all, be his secret goal anyway: Chris feels very comfortable being alone.

We drive out past the Southern Michigan Prison, the largest walled prison in the world, our town's dubious claim to fame. Chris is a guard at the prison. Another place where you stand around with a gun and wait. Chris has a deal with some farmer, so he assures me that the heavy-drinking, holiday-hunter yahoos won't be close enough to nail us when they take aim at just any old moving thing.

*♫.*

Fifteen years before, all it took was for the bear to move, and I pulled down my trusty AK-47, aimed, and blasted. I didn't even think, because all I knew was that I had to protect a dozen kids from the forces of nature, red in tooth and claw, and here it was, a big black bear, attacking! It reared up, it roared, I shot, it fell, the children were safe.

At least that was going to happen, I'm sure, if I'd dawdled a second. What actually happened was that a medium-sized black bear shuffled lazily out of the woods after its own Thanksgiving dinner of old fish guts and heads, discarded on the shore of the river by a small salmon-canning family. It probably didn't even live long enough to know there were kids around.

As for the kids, I sent them home with Idamay. What if it were still alive, playing dead like we've always seen in the monster movies, ready to take out just one last victim? This bear, however, had been ripped open by the force of a military assault weapon, and the force had suitably spoiled the bear as any sort of useful meat, pelt, or tallow, as it was explained to me by the disappointed owner of the gun. Bears are not worth killing so late in the summer because their guts are all a-rot with fish heads and other undigested garbage. The rip in the fur made it equally stinky.

Instead of being the intrepid hero, I was a cad. There is no gain in that kill, except to say, *there, call me a sissy all you like, but I killed a bear.*

I don't think my brother would be impressed by that kill either. No tracking, no skill, no interest, really. When we were boys and apt to kill each other, Chris would spend hours at the lake baiting and casting a half dozen fishing rods, and not receive a single nibble; I'd throw out a line just for kicks and pull out a bass, the way nongamblers pick up a lottery ticket because it comes with a gas-tank fill, and win a hundred bucks.

I'm hoping the same thing will happen today, as we tramp through the frosty woods of rotten brown leaves and bare branches. It's three in the afternoon, but the sun is weak on this late November day and we only have an hour or two of light.

In the gloaming, Chris shows me how a space of earth has been cleared and over it, there are low branches. "There are always low branches. A buck did this," he explains, and he might as well be Leatherstocking, the way he oozes natural authority, "and the doe will come and piss here, as a signal that she's around." I would never have noticed. Then he points to a place up in a tree, and I'm startled to spot a contraption clearly man-made. It's called a "see," and my brother orders me to climb up. It's not as easy as it looks, and my boots are too big for me, so they catch precariously on the half-assed wooden rungs that lead up. Hunting is also a chance for men to relive the glory days of building a cool fort. When I'm situated, I have a strap to clip onto my belt for safety. I use it.

Below, my brother seems tiny in the vast bowl of crumpled brambles. The woods are not lovely, dark, and deep at this time of year; most people abandon the forest after fall foliage season. It seems that this is now my brother's private harsh domain, a place he runs unchallenged. I see a bit of ribbon tied around a branch, footprints. Chris is wandering away with his gun, and I also feel abandoned. *The Blair Witch Project* comes to mind. My nose is running like that girl's. Are there any leftover bad feelings between my brother and me? Not on my part—although I wish he didn't listen to Rush Limbaugh on the radio, that lard-ass.

We are not completely alone. In the distance, we can hear the occasional muffled pop of a rifle going off—once, twice, thrice, and a moment goes by before the fourth. It's like hearing other people in a vast room yelling, "Bingo!" when all you needed was B-21 to win. They got their deer, where is ours? On the road from the airport, in my mother's garden, in the lot behind Uncle Jimmy's house.

I don't know the name of the tree that supports me, I think, not without its leaves to distinguish it. A jay, an arm's length away, mocks me: this is its anonymous tree. "You've got to sit real still," Chris instructs, as he walks further away, "and watch."

"Is this what you do?" I say. Sit still for hours? This is when hunters contrive a reason to drink, smoke, play cards—

the *not* hunting of the hunt. But not my brother. He shrugs when I ask him about it: "I read. I think. And watch. Don't forget to watch."

My brother must have a mind of Zen, clear, at least, compared to mine, which buzzes restlessly like a city intersection. The deer could smell my urban pong a mile away.

I see Chris settle on a log. The gun is slung behind his back, so in my mind, he is suddenly a holy man, with his patience and wisdom and a quiver full of golden (and silver, and pink) magic arrows and an ability to sit still. I think of Saint Eustace, the pagan who hassled early Christians until he wandered into the woods and had a vision of Christ on the cross between the antlers of a deer, resulting in his immediate conversion and a very spiffy logo for the folks who bring you Jagermeister.

The bear I killed to no end has actually haunted my dreams, like Saint Eustace's vision, for fifteen years. I used to wake up and dismiss it as guilt, but as years go by, the bear has become part comforting father figure and part witness. It sits for most of the dream and doesn't move. He is hunting me. That place was his domain. The domain has moved into my dreams. Oh, let me say it: he is godlike. It seems so possible, when I have come into somebody else's realm like this, the realm that belongs to my brother, that I might also be visited by a waking vision.

My brother, after all, has had visions: he saw a deer whose leg had broken and heeled completely over, only in a wrong direction; he shot an arrow through the massive neck of a great stag he found drinking from a stream—and it looked up at him as if he had tapped it on the shoulder, and it went back to drinking for a minute before crumpling to its knees and dying. Chris said it was as if somebody had just told it some very bad news, and it had to sit down to take it in. There are men I've known who have a similar ignorance of their own pain. While I am more than aware of every hangnail and stubbed toe and those ensuing pains, some men can walk around for a week with a dislocated shoulder or open flesh wound, and seem unaware of it. What they have overcome, rather, is the *fear* of wounds, usually from being around a hospital or a farm, where every day it is illustrated how a wound can both appear and heal.

This loss of fear looks good on Chris. It's not arrogance, but a centered quality that seems spiritual. He seems to see better than I do.

This gaze of man. The old saw goes something like, men *do* while women *are*. And for the most part, I'll buy that. But it seems I want to muddy that pure assessment: men do, but they'd rather not be watched while they're doing it, or at least not while making plans leading up to doing it. A great football play, a wartime blitzkrieg, bringing a massive buck to its knees—what would these moments be if men were not at first hidden in huddles in anonymous uniforms and helmets, squirreled away in a foxhole, undetectable in camouflage up in a see? This is also being a man, this hide-and-go-seek, and in the perfect manly world, a man is utterly invisible, except to himself and his God, his witness.

No, the most macho of men is not the big man, but the one so small he's not seen. We love the way God makes us feel small, but, because he is all seeing, and the most invisible, he is the most macho. I will say it now, and wait for lightning and assassination attempts to strike: God, at least in the half-assed way we conceive of him, is a being who made us in his own image, and he is male, even he-man.

When can a macho man get spiritual? While he's hunting. I have come to my homeland of guns and reactionary conservative politics. I live in San Francisco, where every other car has the Darwin fish, the secular humanist response to the Jesus fish, replacing the Savior's name with that of Darwin, the fish sprouting legs, evolving. In Michigan, a new phenomenon: the Jesus fish eating the Darwin fish, ferocious Christianity. Do they know they are affirming the social Darwin tagline, "survival of the fittest"? My brother will survive. He is fit. When he looks at me, he probably sees me unfit, forever flouncing in tights, hitting fabulous sales at Macy's, the Abel to his Cain—and he is puzzled.

The first two brothers, Cain and Abel, had their share of problems, just like Chris and I. The he-man God is hard to figure out sometimes. He demanded animal sacrifice from his followers. Chris gives animal sacrifice. And I give Him the work of my own hand—fruits and nuts, when the Lord specified a fatted calf or a lamb. I always had trouble with that story, with a sense of justice profoundly predating the Aristotelian unities. But there is nothing really Aristotelian about hunting or sacrifice, and there's nothing, therefore, very redemptive, which is the place where we always criticize a work of art, whether we're conservative or radical. It might be that God is not only a he-man, but an Old Testament Guy at that.

In any case, I didn't do anything the He-Man God told us all to do: didn't go forth and multiply, didn't give animal sacrifice, didn't at all understand why he did all those mean things to Job. I may have wanted to kill my brother, but not because his sacrifice was more perfect—it was just that he kept going into my room without my permission. Chris worships that God. By dedicating myself to a life of art, I worship the God of the Enlightenment. Every day white guys across the country struggle with the paltry rewards of living right, making animal sacrifice, getting a ball-and-chain wife, and voting Republican, and grow more and more furious with those of us who prance off to San Francisco or wherever, and don't make the proper sacrifices. When God does not smite the likes of me, people the likes of my brother grow puzzled, disappointed, and poof!—Rush Limbaugh's got six million listeners, and old traditional ways are held even more closely in a rapidly changing world.

Hunting is an old traditional way. It's no coincidence that hunters are religious. The Vendekemp Lake Deli, Bait, & Hunting Supply shop sells copies of *The Camouflage Bible* stacked neatly over a glass case full of pistols. Ted Nugent, the rock star who lives down the road from my brother and is a mover and shaker in the local chapter of the ironically named Ducks Unlimited, is as conservative as they come. Not long ago, he was kicked off the KISS reunion tour for bitching about Latino people not speaking English in America, God's Holy Land. That may be the Lord's desire, but clearly, this is not the message KISS wants to send. All of The Nuge's words give him the fervency of a born-again missionary. The older I get, the more I realize that people who spend a lot of time thinking about human morals *should*—to keep themselves in line. Let the Jesus fish eat the Darwin fish, let Ted speak English to an unlimited number of dead ducks. We will all be better off.

$$\text{ቧ.}$$

That said, my brother's own religious state is much more private, much less proselytizing. He is, essentially, a guy at peace with himself, and I am often envious of his life—a beautiful, smart, and charming wife, two good kids, trustworthy friends, a steady job, and a hobby, for Christ's sake. He is a rare sort: a man who knows what he wants. And he's willing to sit on a cold November day, on a wet log, *for hours*, to wait for it. I look down on him from the see and think about that.

My brother Chris is still, the forest is still, no animal stirs. I do my best to join them. The secret of good storytelling is leaving things out as well as putting things in. This hunt is mostly lack of movement, swift or otherwise. Hunting is being a man at his most manly—not because of the power plays or blood lust so much as the way men assume an inert position and become all watcher, all objectifier, all invisible. Sure, me too: I wanted to clamber out of the tree, but I could not climb down from this see too quickly, for I'd fall to my death. Another good reason to learn how to sit still.

As the darkness encroaches, the amount of gunfire in the distance increases. It's like closing time in a bar, and all the faces are starting to look prettier: that measly doe you could've wrestled to the ground now seems trophy-worthy. My brother fights this temptation almost daily.

Does Chris get all spiritual when he's out hunting? He'd never call it that. That would be like calling attention to the quarterback before the ball is snapped.

But certainly it is the inactivity, the waiting, the tracking, the *divination*, if you will, that is almost all of what is called hunting, and it's in that time that hunters can't help but think of mortality, whether it's the deer's or their own. People close to animals—not pets, but nameless, un-Bambified animals—tend to have a much more sensible idea about life, or much less fear of it.

We go home empty-handed, and my brother is all apologies. For what, I wonder? I didn't have to shoot a gun and subsequently fall out of the see from rifle kickback, and we did the thing that is 99 percent of the hunting: waiting. And Chris will send me home with all the smoked venison and sausage I will ever want.

We ride in his pristine white pickup truck with a well-mounted gun rack, outfitted for every outdoor activity. He's got the radio tuned to something AM, that spooky band catering to psychotic rants and mariachi music, and he barrels down a dirt road, kicking up dust. And I look down at myself, in camouflage. I look like the kind of guy who kills guys like me. And it suddenly occurs to me: I am comfortable with these shit-kickers. Why? Many years ago, around the time the bear died, the first two people in my family I told I was gay were my crazy Uncle Jimmy (sitting, at this November moment, beside the police CB waiting to hear reports of deer being hit by cars, so that he can rush out and do a favor by taking the carcass off the hands of the authorities) and my brother Chris.

What did they say? Uncle Jimmy shrugged and said, "It takes all kinds to make a world." Chris said, "Nobody has to know, you know." What Chris meant, I think, or hope, is that we must be camouflaged, invisible, in order to see more. These are things people say after they've thought a long time about something, probably while up in a see, waiting for that fourteen-pointer.

Was I hoping to get my ass kicked when I blurted out my inverted nature? I am not sure. I do know that if there are any people in this world who are close to the godlike bear I killed somewhere deep in the Alaskan wilderness fifteen years ago, it would be these guys. They are invisible, observing but not judging, only meeting the realities of living in a world that may truly be full of Old Testament he-man wrath and injustice. Every day I work for that God of Enlightenment, believing justice and civilization will result in fairness. But Chris sits in the woods coming to terms with how unfair the world will always be; he seems to have discussed it with a deer or two.

He let me keep my camouflage pants and a big roll of his best sausage. He also gave me two gaily painted arrows, which look very nice in my little apartment in the city, and he does not need to fear a Cain-and-Abel scenario, for these phallic objects are too festively adorned by my blithesome niece, and they will stand firmly in the way of our mutual ends.

# 2

# VALLEJO KILLED
# THE RODEO STAR

I T'S WEDNESDAY NIGHT AT THE COW PALACE, HOME OF
the Grand National Rodeo, Horse & Stock Show. Smell the
popcorn and manure! The evening's events include Dodge-
truck-sponsored bareback riding, Bass-Tickets-sponsored
bronc riding, Continental-Airlines-sponsored team roping,
and House-of-Seagrams-sponsored bull riding. The less
manly events, like women's barrel racing and the coed reining championship, are tucked in between these Wild, Wild
West shows like poor relations.

I am also less manly, the nub-end of a family that is all
he-man: my grandfather fought at Iwo Jima, my father still
holds sports records at the school that he—and I—attended,
my ex-Marine prison-guard brother kills deer with his bare
hands. My own lack of motor skills, my lazy eye, my low
pain-threshold—oh, hell, my homosexuality—have sidelined
me. I am a watcher, a fan, the way Frederick Exley is in his
book *A Fan's Notes*, rather than a performer: "It was my destiny to sit in the stands with most men and acclaim others.
It was my fate, my end, to be a fan." Don't think of me as a
*lover* of men—think of me as a *fan* of men.

Why would a city sissy want to go to the rodeo? Especially now that they have removed the margarita slurpee machine from the concessions? To escape irony. San Francisco, where I live, is eye-roll country, and if you don't believe me, I dare you to come out to the coast and just try— just *try*—to sing the whole national anthem without giggling.

They don't giggle during the national anthem at the rodeo. Every head is raised high, flag level (or in some cases, big-banner-for-Skoal level), belting it out. This is America, dammit, home of the brave, don't you go snickering at my stars and stripes, little mister. What is ironic, however, is that the crowd is a mix of Latinos, African Americans, Filipinos, Asians. The subcontinental lady next to me has a lovely sparkly bindi, and half of me is hoping that Cody Lee from Tucson won't take a spill off Hocus Pocus while the other half is praying my seatmate won't spill her loose-meat sandwich on her saffron-colored sari. Whiteys like me are a clear minority, at least in the stands. The rodeo is recognized around the world as quintessentially American, embodying a romantic notion of the West, and maybe all these folks want to be privy to and possibly part of that fantasy.

I've come before on Latino family night, which is different; everybody waits around after the insane thrill of the very wrong, very amazing "Toro Teeter-Totter" (a bull tries to gore four guys on a set of crossed teeter-totters; each participant depends upon the guy on the other end of the fulcrum to whisk him above, out of horns' way) to hear the musical stylings of Vicente Fernandez, who comes out on a magnificent, unflappable white stallion in the sombrero *gigante y ridiculoso* he made famous long before Chevy's began humiliating its *cumpleanos* customers with its shabby replica. He sings on that horse, and kisses young girls, who rush at him despite the scary body/pony guards, despite the whole problem he's had with thugs who kidnapped his singing son and cut one of his fingers off, despite the fact that he must be pushing seventy. The point is that most of the actual spectators at the rodeo are blacks, Latinos, city slickers.

The cowboys, however, are preposterously white (as if we were the only ones to Go West), with names so bland they're interesting: Cody Custer, JC Sanders, Joe Beaver. There's one black cowboy in the calf-roping event, Texan Fred Whitfield. Later, out in the rodeo mall, among the giant belt buckles and the T-shirts that read, "Cowboy Foreplay: Get in the Truck" and its female counterpart, "Cowboys Are Terrible in the Sack Because They Think 8 Seconds Is a Long Time to Ride," I found that year's Ropers and Riders Pro Rodeo Calendar, full of humpy cowboy dudes looking all sensitive and shirtless. And there was Fred Whitfield, a little bit token, Mr. July. (He has a nice body, by the way, but I prefer Lan La Jeunesse, Mr. October.)

My friends Captain Zap, Martha, Will, Jill, and Owen have come out West too, on their own, separately. Jill, the level-headed Iowan, came to be a country-western music star. Martha moved from Boston to be a journalist. Will is studying to be an economist. Zap came to . . . oh I don't know . . . scuba dive, skydive, and be a horse whisperer back in the stables. The Village People sang, "Go West," and so he did. Owen comes from a wandering family, and when you coax it out of him, he'll tell you about hunting kangaroo with the Maori, or the pet monkey named "Oy Vey" who prefigured him as a beloved child in his parents' life. Almost everybody I know is from someplace else.

We New Westerners are always eager to describe things around here—even when we're watching the same thing, Jill will give her two cents' worth. It's as if we're all writing letters back home. Whether the person was among the early visitors of the Golden West—John Muir, Bret Harte, Mark Twain—or ones who moved here last week, the sense of "here" and "there" never quite disappears. Here, they say, it quakes. There, we all say, it snows. And no matter how many people have gone to the West, they write as if they were the first to stumble upon El Capitan in Yosemite or that great burrito stand in San Francisco's Mission District—or the rodeo.

How would I describe it? Frankly, here at the Cow Palace, all these cowboys milling around outside the ring look like they might show up at the Rawhide (or some other gay Western bar) later on, shoehorned into their requisite Wranglers, combing their droopy mustaches. You want to run your index finger along the napes of their necks just to feel all that good grooming. The fine line between Castro clone style and good Christian clean living blurs easily. If my brother the hunter has a single goal, it's to blend into the landscape; cowboys, on the other hand, are dandies, dressed up to be looked at. What's the look? The rodeo manliness look is, I realize as the night goes on, stern, subtle, self-effacing, and—fussy.

Of course, "fussy" is a relative term. When I watch Olympic divers and gymnasts being given their scores, I'm often mystified at the rulings judges make. Knowing what's a good move and what's a bad move is half the challenge of spectatorship. At the rodeo, I'm so out of it, I can barely tell the difference between a palomino and a paint. As I watch the reining competition, the horses all seem equally clever to me, but one of them, Peppy Lee Pat, is hailed by the announcer as "a slidin' horse!" Is that a good thing?

Cowboys carry their fussy hair-splittin' perfectionist rules of the game out of the corral and into daily life. For instance, I made my first mistake of the evening by ordering a tequila sunrise instead of a beer. I passed from the bar area through the stables and two men with twenty-five gallons' worth of hat between them looked judgingly down at the maraschino cherry bobbing in the bilge. Memo to self: Frozen drinks equal death.

There are certain places where men are allowed to be fussy. Mixed fluffy drinks are right out, but baseball batting averages (NO! it was .357, not .358!), cigars ("She's got a nice cherry"), and 4x4s (27.5 mpg, an improvement over 27.2 mpg) are all examples of situations when guys can behave positively girlishly. The culture at large gives men so little opportunity for enthusiasm that within the narrow band of permission, there are the minute gradations that must be recognized and honored among them.

We all need some massive high-risk event in our lives in order to have something to parse out like batting averages in the locker room. No, that bass was sixteen inches if it was a foot! Jill and I go back to college days. What has often bound us together is a kind of stupid bravery, the reckless kind that could get you killed, but, if not, will give you plenty of material to spin trumped-up yarns in what is quickly becoming our "reflective years." We in our reflective years, eating tri-tip sandwiches and drinking beer in front of them in their material-gathering years riding the ghastly Toro Teeter-Totter—that's here, that's now. We tell each other, knowledgeably, "That's the stupidest thing anybody has ever done."

Jill and I always trot out that story where we all drank too much and Dave B. drove us out to the ocean in his beat-up convertible with an *open container* and Dave was so gone he *stopped speaking English* and Jessica was throwing whole bottles of *malt liquor* out the side of the car and the *cops came* and told us to *move along* and we shoulda *died* back there!

An idiotic event, and not very adventurous, and yet *there*, we cast our hands toward it like a full house up against your two lousy queens, *there*, we have sown our wild oats. Oh sure, Owen, you killed and ate a kangaroo with aborigines. I suppose there was something dangerous and romantic in that, but big whoop. Captain Zap planted land mines for the army. And the very next day, after this rodeo, Martha, on a press junket, would be allowed to ride a tame bull, and in three seconds flat, she'd be pushed roughly up against a wall and have her arm broken. Something to write home about.

.&

But for cowboys at the rodeo, that's for later. The general noise of the rodeo is macho, puffed up in a silent-but-deadly understatedness. A cowboy at one of the two beef jerky sales venues volunteers to me, while looking down at his feet in an aw-shucks shuffle, "Ah moved from Nevada to Caleefornyee, therebah raisin' the ahh-cue in both states." The self-deprecation had the slightest whiff of insult to it, but it wasn't until I sat down in the arena that I realized that he was referring to *mah* low ahh-cue.

Cowboys have a reputation for being rough and uncomplaining on the range and charming and polite indoors. They must get slightly confused with the indoor rodeo, because they've got to be both tough and soft simultaneously. The rodeo has somehow become a family event, a place where

Skoal and Skittles share the same concession stand. Now the master of ceremonies has to clean up his language or turn mean-spirited barbs into jokes. At one point he mocks an Oregon steer wrestler, Michael Reger, by pointing out that the official flower of his home state is a tulip. Uh, sir? The California state flower is a poppy. *Que es mas macho?* Is there such a thing as a macho flower? And by the way, upon further research, the Oregon state flower is the Oregon grape. Maybe Caleefornyins do have a low ahh-cue.

The master of ceremonies later tells the crowd that Heat Rash, a particularly ornery bronc, will "test the eggs." That means: "She's a ball-breaker," which can't be said because after all this is a family event, none of that gutter talk in front of the kids. But does he realize he's comparing male testicles to female ovaries?

Androgyny is everywhere, especially in these macho places. The more manly a man is, the more of a woman he is. What do I mean by that? It's traditional for women to be noticed and admired. Today the cowboy gets to be noticed. And do we watchers—oglers, really—get off so easy? Hell, in a fit of self-reinvention over in the rodeo mall, I just bought a way-too-expensive Resistol cowboy hat I'll probably never wear again, and I feel like a young bride, sipping my drink, hoping I look pleasingly discerning and attractive. Think of this act of watching and not acting as the female advantage, for women are the more alert of the two sexes, and it's only when men are in action that other men are given full license to look at them. Men without motion are invisible men, at least, that is, to men, which makes most men blind most of the time.

.ß.

Look at me, how athletic and dexterous I am, proclaim soldiers, tennis pros, and action movie stars. While women are free to appraise other women with the same zeal that men do, the male gaze is generally forbidden to rest upon another man, but if he's doing something rough and tumble—tackling the quarterback at the Super Bowl, climbing a greased obelisk at the Naval Academy, screwing a chick in a porno movie—then go ahead, dudes, check it out! Feel sorry for us, ladies, for it's only when we're in ridiculous or near-death situations that we rise to your level, only momentarily complete human beings, both surveyors and surveyed.

Everywhere I look at the rodeo, there is that androgynous sheen. The horses themselves are at once muscular and sleek, simultaneously masculine and feminine. During the event called "reining," a kind of horse-dance and western form of dressage, the rider makes the beast spin in quick circles on its two hind legs, and I think of Dorothy Hamill on ice—the more strict the parameters to masculine maneuvers, the more elegant and less manly those maneuvers are. Think of the dainty ballet of a basketball layup, the fey snap of the wrist when the pitcher throws a curve ball. The rodeo is a series of events that are a theme and variation on control. A control over nature, as personified in the beast. A cowboy's scores, his successes, his very pleasure depend upon the horse or the cow or the bull that shake down or kick up, charge, bridle, gore. The calf, lassoed and roped on its side like a beached whale, eyes bulging, seems more puzzled than humiliated: "What? What the fuck did I do?"

I'm the thing that's wrong here. I am giving the little baby cows voices. I am seeing the world through pink-colored glasses. I am looking for irony. Why, oh why, I lament, doesn't the Cow Palace look like Versailles? Do these guys know what some people do with whips and belts? Some men indulge in a pastime called "barebacking," but nobody cheers them on for a seven-second ride. To a sidelined observer, the world is fraught with meaning. The bull called Wango Tango comes flying out of the chute, the loudspeaker blares, and The Village People are singing, "Mah-cho, mah-cho man!"

The music that accompanies bronc and bull riding is the kind of stuff you heard at the roller rink when you were a teenager—"She's a maniac, maniac on the floor," "Hang on Sloopy," "Bad Boys, whatcha gonna do?" This is macho humor. "That steer went straight to Burger King!" says our MC. It's manly understatement, like when "Charlie Too-Tall," the midget rodeo clown yells, "Here kitty, kitty" to the wild bull. This is when manly men are allowed to laugh. They name the bulls "Workmen's Comp," "Crash Landing," and "Sweet Revenge."

We spectators are also meant to laugh at the rodeo clowns, or, as rodeo companion cowgirl Jill calls them, The Depressed Clowns with a Death Wish. If you've never been to the rodeo: the role of the clowns is to deflect the attention of a mad bull after a cowboy has been tossed off its back. They do this with crazy antics, cruel jokes, and the occasional red hanky. Camille Paglia says a homosexual is not a feminine man, but a man taking masculinity to extremity. In the rodeo clown, I find that masculinity-in-extremity Paglia was talking about. For the clowns are risking their lives just as much as the cowboys—perhaps more—and yet they are relatively invisible, hidden behind makeup. They don't give prizes to the best clown, you don't go home with "Charlie Too-Tall" on the tip of your tongue. Their names don't appear in the program.

Think of it: a rodeo clown hides under goofy clothes and a painted smile, but, other than a flimsy barrel sponsored by Dodge trucks, they are utterly exposed to bulls, broncs, and ridicule. They cannot even hide behind the huge muumuu of macho, for when they perform some life-threatening feat or protect a thrown cowboy, the crowd doesn't say, "Boys will be boys"—they say, "That was stupid." A rodeo clown, like a gay man, can't make mistakes and blame them on his gender; each clown is personally answerable for his own dopey mistakes. The Grand National Rodeo keeps an ambulance on hand just in case.

No matter how much the rodeo tries to clean up its act for the children, there is something diabolically awful about some of the events that simply can't be soft-pedaled. For instance, the horrifying yet mesmerizing bull-riding event, appropriately the finale of practically any rodeo, since it often ends in blood and guts and that would, like, totally bogue a seven-year-old's party head. This way parents can remove their kids from the scene or bank on a child's minuscule attention span. Bull riding is one of those things like motorcycles, the right-to-bear-arms amendment to the Constitution, and cell phones that, had we known their impact years down the road, would have been made illegal. But Pandora's box has been opened, and nobody can stop a man from mounting twenty tons of insanity and trying to hold on with one hand. In bull riding, the cowboy wraps his hand several times with the rope bridling the bull, so that when he is thrown, he's still attached to the monster, and the rodeo clowns have to work hard to distract it while the rider is dragged around and tries to untangle his hand from the rope. So not only are the clowns called dopey, but they have to cover for some other nut's dopeyness. *That* is ironic.

♣.

If you've ever been to the gay rodeo, you might find a little more irony, but what you'll really discover is a massive expansion on the pride of the rodeo clown. From the very beginning of a gay rodeo, there's a clownish feel. A gay rodeo opens with the confusingly poignant yet kinda hilarious Ceremony of the Riderless Horse, in which a scary drag queen leads a horse around the arena to represent all of the gay cowboys who have died of AIDS. The events at the gay rodeo are similar to those found at the Grand National—saddle bronc riding, calf roping, barrel racing—but there's also the "Steer Decorating" event, the "Put the Boxer Shorts on the Goat" competition, and a twist on the team roping competition called a Wild Drag Race involving a calf, a gay man, a dyke, and a drag queen. Oh, sure it's funny—until somebody breaks a heel.

Actually they can break a lot more than heels. Thom Sloan, the International Gay Rodeo press relations guy, told me, "Oh yeah, that Wild Drag Race causes quite a lot of injuries." It's hard, after all, to run fast in a dress. Sloan adds, "A friend got gored in the Steer Decorating contest last week in San Antonio, the horn narrowly missing his femoral artery. And there was even a guy who broke a bone in the relatively safe goat dressing event." But that, apparently, was because he was a spaz and fell down.

There isn't a gay rodeo association in San Francisco anymore. It moved down to San Jose half a decade ago due to lack of interest around here. Perhaps we can chalk it up to the triumph of PETA and other animal rights organizations, or perhaps a general sensible love of life and limb.

Gay rodeo participants are often in it for the role playing —doctors and lawyers by day, Marlboro men on the weekends—but some of them are also in pro events like the Grand National. If you asked me to line these guys and their Grand National counterparts up and pick out the gay ones, I don't think I could do it. Each is as tough and dandified as the next. It's all one big fabulous theatrical production.

.&

Rodeo organizers can stick in as many petting zoos, cotton-candy machines, and decorative Arabian horse shows as they want, but what folks come to see—what doesn't bore the kiddies—is pure danger.

It's the same old question—why do we put our lives on the line? But the question endlessly nags at me. Watching people taking nutty risks is inexhaustibly thrilling. As novelist Julian Barnes observed of sex: "A thousand orgasms does not dull the interest in the thousand-and-first." Every time a man on a bull springs from behind a gate, I am shaking my head and saying this is wrong, wrong, wrong. But there I am, peering through my fingers.

It's romantic, a morality play in which a single guy pits himself against the elements. Well, it's not always called romantic. There's the fight against nature and then there is what is called the unnatural, the label queers often get. But being queer requires the bravery and passion of the lone cowboy, and the gumption to confront the cultural beast. Like rodeo clowns, however, homos never get credit—and if they're lucky, they'll only get a good laugh.

In the Cow Palace, the low-key cowboys make it look like all this effort is no big deal. They wear crisp white dress shirts while they rassle steers to the ground (which reminds me of the time somebody crocheted white pot holders for me). Every effort is made by cowboys to make it look effortless, even the way they sit *in* the horse, rather than on it, the way British riders do. Outside, while journalist Martha negotiates tomorrow's ride on the "tame" bull that will break her good writing arm, I watch a dozen white stallions run out a gate to the trailer that will convey them back to the ranch or the next rodeo arena, and I almost forget we're smack in the middle of the overcrowded city. I bet even the horses think they're free for a moment, and this is a grassy valley instead of a parking lot and that, over there, that's not a battered defunct drive-in movie screen serving as the sunset they're riding off into.

I love the rodeo because I, too, am a reckless man. I confine most of my foolhardy behavior to unmonitored gossip and setting expensive vases at the corners of tables where they are most likely to atomize, but watching the cowboys and wearing my brand-new Resistol, I feel a kindred spirit. Recklessness is hardwired in me, and it has led me to the Wild West, led me to the rodeo, risked my health, sanity, and savings account. It will probably be the death of me, but the terms of anybody's demise always seem to be home grown, raised from the raw mental and meat material we get early on, whether it's inherited heart disease or the lazy eye that keeps me clumsily bashing myself into walls and through life. Whether I am stupid or heroic is the fussy call the rodeo judge, or God, will have to make.

I imagine a job for myself at the rodeo. No, not a roper, no, not a clown. Working in the jerky booth seems dull; the margarita machine is gone. Then, just before the event called the Hackamore Triumph (steering a horse with the simplest of reins), a guy comes riding out on a small tractor with a big dragging implement used to smooth out the ruts in the arena. It's the dirt Zamboni. It's mesmerizing too, but in a different way. It's like watching the janitor in high school throw down his orange-red sawdust and then sweep it back up again. I'm not alone in this. The kids behind me, who were obviously bored by events like reining, are riveted by the dirt Zamboni. This is the job for me, down in the rink, in the public eye, the same place where slavering beasts come to gore guys. Look at me! Round and round I go, I'm clearing the corral for the next event, the endless cycle of man versus nature.

# 3

# TAMMY AND THE BACHELOR

FOR A WHILE THERE, I HAD LOST PRACTICALLY everything, including a little mental stability, in a gay divorce, and found some of my queer friends callously unsupportive: accustomed to a revolving-door policy on relationships, they had no way of sounding out the depths of commitment. "Stop acting crazy," they said. "Get over it." My straight male friends, however, had a better guess. They wanted to know why I hadn't broken anything, why there was no bodily harm. For so many reasons, I have preferred the company of straight men.

Which may be why I was quick to volunteer to throw my friend Owen's bachelor party, even though I was Father of the Bride and not Best Man. The best man lives in Los Angeles, and while it is his traditional duty to facilitate the groom's one last moment of freedom, it was easier for me to arrange things as co-thrower. I would make the invitations, for I am *fabulous* with invitations. Glen, the real best man, would do the programming. I saw the whole thing as a grand experiment: what do boys do when grouped together and encouraged to behave lasciviously?

But alas, this was not a valid experiment. First of all, we live in San Francisco, the home of *sensitive* men. Second, I

was monitoring the affair and they knew I was, and therefore, the uncertainty created under the auspices of the
Heisenberg principle disqualifies the study: for the observer
always changes the observed, and the more accurate the
observation of one aspect of an experiment, the less accurate will be your observation of its other aspects.

Third, Owen and the rest of us are in our thirties, not
twenties, when wild oats are traditionally sown. We go to
bed around midnight during the week, and have learned the
fine art of "chemical bracketing"—maintaining a buzz of
whatever sort without drinking or doping to the point of losing control of bodily functions. "I've tried whiskey, cocaine,
ecstasy, and designer drugs, but I got left behind when I Said
No to crack," somebody at the party philosophized. We are
all post-crack babies. (At a Moby concert, where I was the
oldest person by ten years, a groover boy came up to me
waiting for friends by the Moby Screen Saver booth, and,
seeing me mesmerized by the pretty undulating colors on
the sample computer screen, asked me, "Hey man, do you
have a K connection?" and, my mind on computers at the
moment, I replied, "You know, I don't even have DSL.")

All of us except maybe Stinky Stanley, former Golden
Gate Park bush dweller, short-order cook, and gravel-voiced
friend of the groom. Stinky, who would later be deputized by
the County of San Mateo for twenty-four hours in order to
hitch Owen and his sweet cowgirl bride, Jill, together, had
great concern that a properly raunchy evening might not
occur. He was, perhaps, correct. After all, I'd never been to a
bachelor party before, only heard about them—the girl
jumping out of the cake, the drinking too much.

What, I wondered, is the gay equivalent of a bachelor
party? Every party is a bachelor party, unless you're foolish,

reckless, or romantic enough to get yourself into a long-term relationship.

For the record, Owen was dragged kicking and screaming to his own party. "Can't we just go bowling or something?" he wanted to know. His brother Joe told me that Owen has a mortal fear of two things in this world: strippers and skeletons. I promised Owen I'd do my best to keep the bachelor party skeleton-free.

We were jealous of the bachelorette party, where they had a cake and gift bags from Crabtree & Evelyn, and a trip to the Saddlebag in San Jose, where the belt buckles are plate-sized and the girls wear cowboy boots and tan panty hose, and where they all rode the mechanical bull in dresses (which many of the boys perhaps would have preferred as a peep show). It would also be the place where our friend Martha would get bitten by the bull-riding bug, leading to the aforementioned broken arm.

I didn't dismiss bowling outright. Or at least something to do with bowling balls. It seems that Stinky had just returned from another wedding in his native Keokuk, Iowa. At the bachelor party there, the main event did not involve girls in Pasties of Abnormally Large Size (PALS) or Straps of Incredibly Small Proportions (SISPs), but a hastily constructed cannon that shot a bowling ball skyward with the help of a great deal of loose black gunpowder. "It was incredible!" Stinky reminisced in a voice tempered by cigarettes, bourbon, and Iowa, while we all gaped in imaginative appreciation. "It would get so high up in the air that it looked about as big as a golf ball, and then when it came down, no matter where you were standing, you were sure it was heading right for you."

Well, why couldn't we shoot bowling balls off? "Aww, Brian," Stinky waved me off. "Nobody asks questions about gunpowder in Iowa. You just tell folks you're gonna blow a stump outta your yard or something, and they just give it to you. Here in San Francisco, shit, people ask questions."

The Right Reverend Stinky essentially saved the party from my queeny efforts to *dramatize* and *thematize*: he was the first to arrive at my house, carrying his trademark briefcase. For this occasion, he had a bottle of fine tequila, six limes, four porno tapes (disguised porno; the Tracy Lords video was labeled *Helicopters of the Vietnam War*), and five packs of Merit cigarettes. At the wedding, I saw him with a draft of the wedding vows and a Max Brand western: *Ripon Rides Double*. And only four packs of Merit cigarettes. I admire Stinky for not saying anything about my Tuscan tile floors or matching bowls for chips and Cheetos. He walked right past the handmade dulcimer and the manicured dozen roses in a vase, announced "I've brought porn—old school and new school!" and commenced chopping up limes for the tequila.

New school, he explained, involves puppies and vegetables.

He was not kidding. As the twenty-plus cowboy guests sauntered in with six-packs of Budweiser, Stinky orchestrated an evening-long crescendo of smut for us. We started with Betty Page's *Teaserama*. She's the queen of old school. When they transferred the Betty Page films to video, in a number of places they cut off the models' heads at the top of the screen— in order to make sure that the gams are fully displayed at all times. Betty Page is sweet burlesque. In one long sequence, she carefully dresses up a fellow model in corset, shoes, and elbow-length gloves. "My God," said Glen, the best man, "they're not undressing, they're dressing! That's kinky!"

One of the guys brought over some vintage porno magazines including some 1975 *Playboys* as well as fetish items like *Smart Asses* and something involving girls in bikinis fighting. This distracted everybody from commenting on my matching bowls.

The subject of body hair came up and gay and straight bonded for a moment—we all agreed that Nair was way too overused in the porno industry. Stinky described a pretty Armenian porn star lady named Crystal Breeze, who did not shave anything. Owen, the groom, narrowed his eyes at Stinky. "Breeze is *not* an Armenian name." Owen was chemically bracketed.

Then there was *Pig*. I won't go into it, except to say that it is not *Babe*. *Pig* would not have been half so disturbing had it not been a twelfth-generation tape of the original; it had the grit and mood of the Roswell alien autopsy film.

There were many astute observations made at this untypical bachelor party. There were knowing discussions of dyke wildwoman writer Jeanette Winterson, and the best man and I discussed Iris Murdoch.

Nevertheless, these were men, together, without women. We discussed NASCAR, and Owen received a spelunker's headlamp for the field trip to the Mitchell Brothers strip club later that evening. The toilet seat was up the *entire* time. And when Glen had us all gather around to hear a reading from Alice Sebold's beautiful and disturbing memoir, *Lucky*, a book about experiencing and surviving rape, we all knew the importance of stopping somewhere prior to the Mitchell Brothers, to think about women. We thought it would be good to have a big group hug.

But there was no group hug. There's only so far men will go. We all liked the concept, but get real. Honestly, I only wanted a Kodak moment. Instead of the group hug, somebody pulled the little plastic lemon out of my refrigerator and squeezed the juice out of it, imitating the act of orgasm, or some other loss of bodily functions.

Men, even San Franciscan men, even gay San Franciscan men, have to work hard to find ways to show emotions. Folks will consider you a sissy or a lunatic if you show any feeling at all. So what do guys do to show tenderness? Sometimes they end up generating incongruous, weird ways to express their emotions. In a recent issue of *Lowrider* magazine, I noted that a grieving father had built a garish airbrushed car as a memorial to his infant son. I saw on the back of a pickup with a "Real Men Love Jesus" bumper sticker, the pirated image of Calvin, usually depicted pissing into the gas tank, shown bowing reverently before the crucifix, in a twisted version of the icon of Santa Cruz. In a similar way, we sandwiched the reading from *Lucky*, about terrific violence against women, into an evening full of exploitation. It was a wrenching but real effort to remind ourselves that we are connected to a world that is incongruously both grippingly awful and dumbfoundingly hilarious.

Once we'd all been chemically bracketed, we removed ourselves to San Francisco's venerable Mitchell Brothers Theater, the crème de la crème of strip joints. What did I expect? Something more down-at-heel. If the boys were disappointed that my bachelor pad was not more bachelorpaddy, they must have been destroyed by the slick cleanliness of Mitchell Brothers. It was downright fussy. Let me just say that gay strip shows are not this fabulous.

The truth is, the Mitchell Brothers is, well, kind of faggy. More disco than you'll ever hear at Pleasuredome, the mostly gay SOMA dance club. The main stage is like a runway, with fashion out the wazoo. My gay pal Blake pointed out a woman who'd traded up her Cruella DeVille dalmatian coat for what can only be described as the outfit for a south-of-the-border devil Sherpa—something drag queens might wear. When she bent over in our gay faces, Blake gave me a puzzled look and murmured, "Something's missing."

There were a lot of gender-bending moments here—a crack team of strippers known as "T&A Construction," girls with neutral names like Morgan and Kim. The Copenhagen girls performed a lesbian love act in the Ultra Room after a brief performance on the stage and a mad, game-showlike scramble for the dollars thrown toward them.

And another gender swap: the "no hands" rule. The women can touch the men—indeed, if you pay enough, the women will unzip the men. We can pretend that this rule is for the safety of the women, but get real: just as the bachelor party is meant for the rest of the menfolk and not the bachelor, who'd rather be bowling, the "no hands" rule is for the benefit of the menfolk, not the ladies. What better fantasy in the world than to have the girl do all the work, all flamenco hula hands and enthusiasm?

What if I told you that the whole idea behind a bachelor party is to get in touch with the feminine side? We had this particular bachelor party, anyway, to comfortably enjoy the company of the same sex, to say "ewww" when the man's penis erupts in a porno, to discuss sports statistics with fussy accuracy, to smoke cigars and ignore their phallic shape, and to keep our hands at our sides and pretend to let somebody else do the lusting. And finally, whether we wanted it to or not, the bachelor party was held to find some way, however disguised, of recognizing the need to feel something, and then celebrating those feelings—by seeing how desperate and lonely we are, gay men and straight alike—without the company of women, without true love. In the morning, we all got up off the floor and apologized to one another. I made coffee.

A week later, Owen was married. The bride wore cowboy boots. And when she threw the garter to the bachelors, it was coming right at me, but Glen the best man nearly knocked me down in order to snatch it from this bachelor's hands.

# 4

# MONSTER

IN THE DENTIST'S WAITING ROOM, THE CHOICES ARE *Highlights for Children* or a fashion magazine. Since I lost interest in *Highlights* when it stopped running the delightfully grotesque comic about the lumberjack Timbertoes family (those half-human, half-wooden cousins of Pinocchio —they scared and intrigued me at once), I flipped through a section of beauty tips in *Vogue*.

"Most women," reads an offhand statistic, "look at themselves in a mirror an average of eleven times a day."

I do not claim to be anything remotely close to a typical man, but I think I can safely say that, if this little nugget is even slightly truthful, there are some huge differences between me and women.

I hate to look at myself in the mirror. Call it low self-esteem if you want, but really, really, there is very little of interest for me to look back at from a reflective surface. I have lived with this face all my life, and there are very few surprises left. I have even perfected the art of shaving in the shower, mirrorless; in fact, I find on those rare occasions when I do shave with a mirror, I cut myself.

This is yet another way I differ from many gay men, who crave beauty with voraciousness nearly insatiable, and the

desire to attract attractiveness is turned in on itself in order
to create the most effective mantrap possible.

🥾

It is the summer before I am to be in the third grade and
it's swim period at day camp. I love Clark Lake, the big dock,
the sandy bottom, the tall yellow lifeguard chair, the line of
buoys that may as well demarcate the end of the earth.

I love to swim and would later become a lifeguard, a
swim instructor, despite (or perhaps because of) one thing:
I have to wear a bathing cap. Yes, "because of": there is nothing like difficulty and impediment to motivate me to
surmount difficulty and impediment.

The year before, the mastoid process in my right ear
(that's the anvil of the hammer and anvil) got so infected
that they had to surgically remove it. The surgeon sliced
through my eardrum in order to get at the rotten thing in
me, diminishing my hearing in that ear by a third (and
despite or perhaps because of this, I came to be a music
lover) and forcing me to swim, for the rest of my life, with
extensive protection against wetness in my inner ear. Today
I have clever shape-molding malleable earplugs, necessary
since the surgery also widened the opening in my ear into an
irregular, huge size (roughly the shape of Australia flipped
on its side; over many childhood years I studied that shape
with a combination of bathroom mirror and my mother's
handheld mirror). But back then, I had to make do with a
jerry-rigged combination of cotton, tape, and, oh horrible of
horribles, a bathing cap.

Not a slick groovy Speedo Olympic number, no. This
was 1971 and all I had available to me was one of my grandmother's fancy caps with layers and layers of latex fringe. It

looked like a cannibalized fetishistic flapper's dress. It was either that or the one that made me look like a hydrangea.

I was treading water and three kids swam up. One of them, dared, said, "We were wondering, are you a boy or are you a girl?"

♫.

The 1976 edition of the *Boy Scout Handbook* had a whole section on puberty. The Magic of Adolescence. There was a series of diagrams showing two or three different body types growing, developing, enlarging. There was an Endomorph, an Ectomorph, and Something In Between. Even at that age I must have known they were throwing me a bone, trying to make me believe there was no such thing as abnormal when in fact they were reinforcing—dictating —the tenets of abnormality.

I prayed to be the example called Something In Between, in every way the physical equivalent of invisible. Stripped, I held the page of the *Scout Handbook* at arm's length, with the mirror facing me, my reflection right beside the picture. If I adjusted my arm just right, I was just as big as the Something In Between Boy in the book. We were both thirteen. Surrounding his outline, however, were the onion layers of his future, a boy at fourteen, at fifteen, and on, which made him seem to be vibrating, sending out secret waves. In any case, he had a trajectory, an ultimate goal, and his body was expanding in the right direction. Did I match him? Were my shoulders as broad? My waist as slim? My penis as big?

"A woman is almost continually accompanied by her own image of herself. Whilst she is walking across a room, she can scarcely avoid envisaging herself walking." That's what John Berger—a man—observes in *Ways of Seeing*.

I, on the other hand, walk across the room and feel perfectly nonexistent. Being neither beautiful nor ugly, fat nor skinny, short nor tall, I remain Something In Between—I blend in. At least, that's what I like to believe: that I can be anonymous, the invisible man.

To what purpose? To spy, to collect information, to observe others—women, men, dogs, decor. It's an artist's job, I tell myself, but what about all those other invisible men who are not artists?

For I believe that many men think they, too, are invisible. Imagine a legion of little boys covering up their eyes with their fat little fingers and hollering to Mommy, "You can't see me!"—and believing it, sincerely.

The invisible-man syndrome may be one of the reasons why so many men have such big, particular problems with ethics. The banker dips his hands into the till, he's unseen. The lawyer puts a pubic hair on a soda can and shows it to a coworker, who'll know the difference? A covert war is started by the CIA. If they thought they were being watched, they'd take the fingers from their eyes.

This ethical problem isn't limited to the obvious crimes of embezzlement, harassment, and war. When in that pivotal third-grade year Joe Dalton lorded over me a hefty piece of pyrite he found in his driveway gravel, he bragged, "This is fool's gold." As if the first word had nothing to do with it, or was in fact something that made it even more valuable. Gold was gold. And Joe impressed upon me that its value was as such, because he wouldn't even trade a whole bag of marbles for it, because are you crazy, it's Fool's Gold—gold that once belonged to a man named Fuhl, or mined from a forty-niner camp near a town called Fulz.

Grown-up versions of Joe Dalton are hard at work, advertising cigarettes with cancer warnings built right in and pushing prescription drugs that are required to list their own terrible side effects. Somehow those ad-men have made the stuff invisible or part of their power.

🥾

Thinking that it might enhance my ethics, I decided to start looking at myself in the mirror as often as *Vogue* said women do—my way of taking my fingers from in front of my eyes. Is my hair sticking up? Are the veins in my temples bulging? Did I miss that spot under my chin while shaving? Are there crow's-feet near my eyes? Frown lines around my mouth?

I'm nearing forty, time to start taking care of my skin. Time to become vain, I guess, when it's a little too late. Frankly I'm thrilled to grow older. Discerning the slow recession of my hairline through a sequence of photographs, seeing the wrinkles, the emergence of cragginess that, well, looks good on men—character, they call it.

These I don't hate to observe in the mirror. It's the less obvious imperfections I see there that I wish I didn't. My chin is my mother's, and, bless her heart, I wish it weren't. The slump in my shoulders comes from my father's side of the family.

I can also see that my right eye is closed more than the left, it's lazy—I spent that same traumatic third-grade year with a patch over the left eye and big dorky glasses to strengthen it, though it turned out to be too late.

Nowadays I have to wear glasses that correct nearsightedness in one eye and farsightedness in the other. The lens in my right eye is demonstrably thicker than the left, and while the eye sleeps, sags, and lazes, its shiftlessness is emphasized by the magnifying lens over it. It is huge, and I can frighten infants with it.

My tongue is also lazy. I can't roll it, or R's, so that I'm shy about learning foreign languages.

It's as if the whole right side of me is a mutant, the reckless Mr. Hyde to an articulate Dr. Jekyll. The diminished sense in my absurdly large-yet-deaf ear, enlarged-yet-blind eye must have something to do with my being left-handed—left-handed, at least, in the dexterous activities like writing, handling chopsticks, and cutting out paper dolls. I still do some things with my right hand, but they are more brutal activities, like batting a baseball, bowling, masturbating. My right shoulder muscles are more solid, overdeveloped. You can't immediately see it in me, but when I look into a mirror, I see a cyclopean, elephant-eared, hunchbacked freak at war with my more gentle, acute, and human aspects. All of those secret things I see in the mirror, and I don't like to be reminded of them.

But it's the handicapping of my senses that has also made me want to be a lifeguard, buy opera tickets, read in dim light on trains. Contrariness has become part of my character.

As I began to check myself the requisite eleven times daily in the mirror, I began to cheat: I wasn't looking at myself in the mirror—I was looking at the mirror itself.

Pretty mirrors, the vanity of vanities! This one has a beveled edge, that one has a flaw in the upper corner, like a healed flesh wound. This one needs resilvering, that one is wreathed by a hand-carved ornamental design of acorns and oak leaves. Georgian, Gothic, bathroom, handheld. The one over a bar, the wall-sized one at the gym or in a ballet conservatory, the one in a small cramped restaurant installed to make the place look bigger, more spacious. These last always throw me—I'm eating and I look across the room to see somebody vaguely familiar. Who is that man with the stooped shoulders and receding hairline?

I have come to prefer the mirrors that distort—not just the obvious funhouse waves that make me a midget or give me a gut, but mirrors hung at a severe angle so that I can see the top of my head or put in an odd light source so that I seem green, or tan, or to have more hair.

We exaggerate and distort a story in order for it to be believed. The grotesque reveals truths.

♫.

When she was in third grade, my friend Libby wanted to be a boy. She had her mother take her to the beauty parlor to get her hair cut off. Her mother said, give her a pixie, the fashion of the early seventies when Olympic star Dorothy Hamill made short hair on girls *comme de garçon*, all the rage.

Her mother was surprised to find at the dinner table that her shorthaired daughter, in overalls, was joined by a brother with a towel wrapped over his head and draped at the shoulder like a pharaoh's headdress. "What are you doing at the dinner table with a towel on your head?" his mom wanted to know.

"If Libby is going to be a boy, then I'm going to be a girl," he said, biting daintily into his bread, a moment just barely imaginable to me, the notions a small boy might have as to how girls were different than boys.

Libby's brother was told—quite fiercely, by father—to take that towel off your head at the dinner table and behave like a boy. Mother was more gentle with Libby and her sex change:

"You can't be a boy."

"Why not? I have a boy's haircut."

Libby doesn't recall the key phrases that convinced her that she could not be a boy, but she understood as much.

"Then I want to be something else, if I can't be a boy."

"What would you like to be?" asked her mother, probably feeling indulgent.

"A monster," said Libby.

.આ

There are monsters that scare me. The Timbertoes from *Highlights*, half-human, half-wood. The Borg from *Star Trek*, half-human, half-machine. The Creature from the Black Lagoon, half-human, half-fish. Neither fish nor fowl, these beings are impure, freakish, one-of-a-kind.

There are other, less-frightening monsters too. Mary Shelley's creature in *Frankenstein*, standing on the ship among the ice floes, alone. Virginia Woolf's *Orlando*, a woman-man who flops from sex to sex like a fish out of water, on through the ages. Jeanette Winterson's web-footed gondolier in *The Passion*. Katherine Dunn's narrator in *Geek Love*, an albino dwarf. And what about Proust, who reportedly switched the sexes of real-life friends and lovers to create the characters of his novels, as easy as flipping burgers on a broiler?

These are monsters I have loved. Women writers are able to create the best of these monsters, though some men have had their successes. Their characters are monsters who tell stories, who have been simultaneously in the margins, invisible, and at the center of attention too. They are object and subject of their own tales, their sight is more sensitive, their bodies more sensual. They are what we mean when we say *androgynous*.

♪.

When I was in the ninth grade, I began to grow a breast. It wasn't surprising to find that it grew under my right nipple. It wasn't what guys in gym class called hermans, ta-tas, winnebagos, but to me, it was huge. It was a lump that compounded my misery: I suspected breast cancer, among the list of other things: hermaphroditism, genetic mutation, homosexuality. Probably few people noticed it, but I couldn't keep my eyes off of it. I studied it in the mirror, poked it, prodded it, squeezed it hoping it would burst like a pimple, but it seemed to be growing larger. Under the soft skin of my nipple, I could feel a buildup of tissue, fibrous, muscular. It seemed some unfinished thing, an incubus, the outer space spore they let develop in a test tube in science fiction movies to see what it will become, until it's too late and it has eaten the lab assistant.

I wasn't going to let it get that far. I called a doctor out of the phone book—not the family doctor—to get it taken care of. I had an after-school job, and I was willing to pay for all medical expenses myself.

It's a hazy memory for me now, except perhaps the exam, the questions. I don't remember what that doctor looked like, though I can remember the location of his office downtown, in an area I considered nondescript, invisible. How did I arrive at this doctor? Did I seek out a breast specialist? Somebody who was good at what I then considered "sex things"? I told him how it had been there for at least a year, and it was getting larger. He said it was rather small, did it bother me, physically? No, I said, but it had begun to secrete a little something, oh God, was it milk? When I wore a T-shirt in gym class, I could see it press against the cotton, and playing shirts against skins in basketball was the most miserable experience imaginable.

I thought of the Amazons, that tribe of women who burnt off one breast so that they could shoot arrows more accurately. The legend of such a race of beings must have terrified men throughout history—a self-sufficient breed who were half-man, half-woman. No men necessary, just drop your sperm at the door, thank you very much, we'll pick it up later. I was an Amazon, a monster, half-man, half-woman.

The removal of the growth was handled very discreetly. It was as if we were all embarrassed by this aberration. My parents were notified by this doctor—he must have coaxed their names out of me—and they did not chastise me or discuss it at any length. They were sympathetic and swift, and I was carted off to the local hospital as an outpatient, where I went under briefly and woke up to find an Ace bandage wrapped several times around my chest: the mummy, unbound.

It was my father who drove me to and from the hospital. He was kind to me, but only asked me if I was in pain, those sorts of questions. And only after the anesthetic wore out did I hurt, that very particular hurt of flesh when it has been cut—it is the sympathy pain I feel when I am told a person has had a sex change, for I know that the dull insistent throb of separated meat on our bodies doesn't abate for a long time.

The incision healed nicely, and now it is almost invisible. If I took the time to study it closely in a mirror, I might see the scar, but you would never see it, not knowing where to look. A modest slice that traced the underside of the aureole of my nipple, needlessly cosmetic since my chest has since grown over with hair. The growth never returned, but I wonder what happened to the original missing piece—did they keep it in a jar to study in a lab? Did they ever discover what it was that made this decidedly feminine thing form on me? Did it have anything to do with my monstrous right side, did I sit wrong in my mother's womb, did I fall into a heap of radioactive debris on that side? Or am I simply a monster?

♪.

Rainer Maria Rilke was obsessed with these monstrous things: transformation, watching, being watched. If I only had a nickel for every appearance of the word "mirror" in his poems. He writes in "Turning-Point" of a man "whose vocation was Waiting" in an anonymous hotel room, avoiding that room's mirror, equally ignorant of his ego with its anonymous reflection: "Learn, inner man, to look on your inner woman, the one attained from a thousand natures, the merely attained but not yet beloved form." There is another Rilke poem in which Rilke (invisible, the observer, male) watches children play with a ball. The ball is bounced about, tossed, adored. It is the object of the children's affection. Their pleasure depends upon it. The ball goes high into the air and Rilke is thrilled to note the situation magically change, if only momentarily: the children, awaiting the ball to reach its apex on the launch, rearrange themselves around the ball, trying to anticipate its return trajectory. Suddenly the subjects become objects—it is the ball objectifying the children.

There are times when I too have turned from subject to object, watcher becoming watched. Certainly, if I do not check myself in the mirror properly, I might go out with a misbuttoned shirt, a tie with a stain. That's one reason why I have a True Love. I need somebody outside of me to observe me, and if not to adore me, then to objectify me, to say, subtly, "Are you going out in *that*?"

But there is just so much scrutiny I can bear before I flee. Under the watcher's eye, I feel like a fourteen-year-old, and it is at that age—when my phantom breast grew—that I wished myself the most invisible. Love is scrutiny, but what will my True Love think when he discovers that I am secretly damaged goods?

And who else watches me? The ones who desire me, I suppose, although they mostly spy, like me. The homeless watch me. On the street, some ask for money, but others say, "Just give me a smile." When I don't smile—because a false, silly smile is called a simper and I don't want to give a simper—I am immediately called an asshole. Women friends say this is what they get from men who say, "Hey, baby doll, give us a smile," as if this were a harmless, unsexual request; they are infuriated when such a tiny gift is denied. "I have gone from 'Little Darling' to 'Bitch' in ten seconds flat," my friend Stephanie tells me.

Some watchers don't understand that the watched are not public property. They don't understand that complete strangers are not to be aggressively insinuated upon, nor touched, as in the case of pregnant women I have seen fondled in supermarkets—even by other women. A watcher must only watch—not insinuate a power over the watched. This is what I fear: the power.

.&.

Who are the emerging paragons of androgyny, the males who yearn for female qualities? Who are the ones who are as brave as women, who do not think they are invisible?

I think they are the vain men, the debonair peacocks, the macho guy with twenty gold rings and a fast flashy car that grabs your attention, the ones who aren't afraid to say,

"Look at me! I'm Baberaham Lincoln!" or, "Look at me, I am one ugly motherfucker!"

There is hope in the new generation coming up behind me. I see fifteen-year-old boys on the beach who are so full of their own beauty, they can hardly find time to be looking out at others. They strut, they let drop an occasional benevolent smile, butter wouldn't melt in their mouths. I have no doubt that they look in the mirror eleven times a day. I see handsome straight men smiling when gay men wolf-whistle, comfortable with their own beauty. Unlike me, they don't mind being scrutinized. They check themselves in the mirror at least eleven times a day.

How could I redeem vanity?

Vanity is more pure than much of what is given that label. I am mildly puzzled by contact lenses that change your eye color, nose jobs, skin peels. These are called acts of vanity but are in fact subtle forms of self-hatred. These things do not highlight one's physical aspects, they hide them as if they were something to be ashamed of. Since when were blue eyes better than brown eyes?

With real vanity comes a self-sufficiency that is momentarily threatening but also magical. When you remove the object of desire, when the self is both watcher and watched, desire itself transforms into something like longing, or nostalgia, maybe, what the Portuguese call "saudade." The one who observes and is observed is also at a standstill—Narcissus gazing into the pool—somebody waiting, unmoving, full of a potential, uncontrollable energy, like the airborne ball in Rilke's poem.

Rilke, again, and finally: "And the rumor that there was someone who knew how to look, stirred those less visible creatures: stirred the women." As I grow older, it becomes more important that I not only learn how to become visible, but that I also learn to see the world through different eyes. Men are at their best when they are uncomfortable—alone, out of the company of other men, out of uniform, forced to be self-sufficient, and perhaps a little frightening, like any good monster. In other words, men are at their best when they rise to the level of women.

# 5

# BLOOD, SWEAT, AND TEARS

"**B**APPITA-BAPPITA-BAPPITA"—THE SOUND OF BOXING is the sound of old Don Martin comics in *MAD* magazine. I'm listening to the "woo-chik! woo-chik! woo-chik!" of incessant jump-roping and the sneezy "snerf! snerf!" sound boxers make, synchronized with their punches. There's a radio tuned to an oldies station playing Pink Floyd's "Comfortably Numb." Here at the M&M Boxing Gym on Harrison Street in San Francisco's Mission District, Sonny Marson and his son Ernie have decorated with old heavyweight match promo posters. I say they'd be better off with rough pine furniture and stiff billowy linens, but maybe that's none of my business.

For fifty bucks a month, guys come here to work out, put on the gloves, shadowbox, work out a little aggression. In this posh town of chrome-and-glass health clubs with track lighting and mouthwash dispensers, M&M is refreshingly basic, and smells like the high school gym: stale sweat, hormones, and towel-snappin' fear and pain.

For the preceding few months, the fear and pain I was enduring was post-boyfriend; it has its own smell, a kind of dumb head-butting stench that makes one hard to be around. The image comes to mind of that adolescent time when my little brother, Scott, just to please his oldest brother, would allow me to take his hand in mine and slap his face while I asked him, over and over, "Why are you hitting yourself? Why are you hitting yourself?" I was tired of that stupid, repetitive pain, and I knew I could find fresh hurt at the fights.

Which is probably one reason boxing hasn't been so popular in San Francisco in the last few years. Attendance at bouts has gone down steadily. Sonny Marson laments, "Now it's white wine and cheese time."

Marson notes that the history of boxing has always been unglamorous. It's a chance for the down-and-out to pick themselves up. The poor can become rich, the loser can become a winner. Paris Alexander, who has fought professionally and comes to the gym to assist in training, is one of Sonny's success stories. Paris says, "Boxing is a little more red-light district than your average sport."

But Paris Alexander, thirty-four years old, doesn't see Sonny's gym as dubious—when I talk to him, he's preoccupied with faith and trust—he trusts Marson implicitly. He's been with Sonny for eight years, and like so many of the guys in here, he's missing one tooth. "I was nineteen when a friend gave me a ticket to the Leonard-Hearns fight in 1982. I was hooked. I won two Golden Gloves titles in 1985 and '86, and then went pro. Went to the Olympic trials. Since then, boxing has helped me travel. I've fought in Denmark, France, Australia, and Vegas." Paris smiles a lot, he seems really happy in this gym. He's done a lot of coaching, especially with white-collar/white-wine-and-cheese guys looking for a workout. Paris is a degreed therapist working with senior citizens and he and his wife have a pretty daughter who models. "But the boxing is the dream," he smiles again.

Boxing is the dream for him, but not for me—I am not into pain, ironic, for the number of clumsy scrapes I've been in. The last time I went to a leather bar it was because I was getting paid to do it, and when some S&M'y guy put a big firm paw on my arm as a coercive come-on, he grabbed me right where my flu shot had been administered, causing me to say something like, "ouchy-ouchy-ouchy," which is, as you can guess, *not* hot, and which ruined my reputation for the night. And as Joyce Carol Oates said in her brainy but humorless book *On Boxing*, "Contrary to stereotyped notions, boxing is primarily about being, not giving, hurt."

So, no thanks, Sonny, please don't ask me to put on the gloves.

♨.

This is not to say I avoid every sort of confrontation. And just because I don't like to get my face bruised doesn't mean I don't care for combat. Any number of battles are waged on a daily basis, most of them losing propositions, and many of them not so obviously bloody, but painful nevertheless.

Take my good friend Hugh, for example, the man who always recommends good novels to me, keeps up on flea market finds, and grows a tuft of soul patch just under his lower lip. He also makes his own low-cut plaid skirts—kilts, if you will. He and his friend Jay used to run around and take on the catcalls and goosings from various Tenderloin hoods and lowlifes. "I figure we look like every librarian who ever threw them out for loitering in the reference room," Hugh once told me.

Jay and Hugh were inseparable for years in San Francisco's wild and woolly days (that would be any day prior to the late Boom Economy). Then Jay got a job in

Portland and moved away. I saw him for the first time in years and he had changed quite a bit from his wild arty days when we used to throw parties where a guy named "Art DeBrix" would crash and my underwear would somehow get stolen. Jay had cut his hair conservatively and let the five piercings in his left ear grow closed again. "You should see the 1966 Marimekko design Hugh found," I told him, "It's blue and yellow, he looks like a demented Cub Scout den mother."

Jay grimaced. "Oh, sure, Hugh can pull that stuff off in San Francisco, but I'd like to see him try that crap in Portland."

The *esprit de l'escalier* consumed me after I walked away, feeling a chill. The thing is, Hugh would wear skirts in Portland, or anywhere, for that matter. It's not about "getting up the nerve," it's not a conflict of courage versus cowardice; Hugh wears skirts because that is how he is, how he has to be in order to be himself, honestly, in whatever world he finds himself.

Dresses look terrible on me; I respect the practice far too much to make a mockery of transvestitism. But in the same way, I am what I am, and part of what I am is a sissy boy far more comfortable around hillbillies and boxers and hunters. I probably look like a goon among the trendy gay boys of San Francisco, and feel more at ease in a sweatshirt and cleats than anything fashionable. What does courage really mean? Overcoming fear, no doubt. But there is no fear involved for Hugh when he dons a dress. Hugh told me, "When I wear a dress, it's not referential to any place, Portland, San Francisco, or wherever. This is who I am, and that's not a variable. Besides, wearing a dress has not made me exactly *happy* to any significant extent."

I don't think men who box are being brave, not exactly. They're not overcoming something they're afraid of. There's something else at work, something hilariously similar to Hugh's need to wear dresses. Boxing doesn't make them happy, to any significant extent, but fosters a transformation, a push toward the redemption of all the daily compromises and self-betrayals—compromises that seem like a form of defeat—that can only be made through a conflict with the world.

*♫.*

Sonny would not ask me to put the gloves on: no dilettantes allowed. And this month, things are downright Oatesian, what with all the serious, *humorless* preparations for Golden Gloves Boxing.

Harrison Street is a fairly new location for Marson and associates, because Sonny had his setup in the Hall of Justice for decades. This ended with the advent of Mayor Willie Brown's administration in 1994, and since then, M&M has struggled to keep things running with the most basic of facilities, like a landed nobleman out of favor with the reigning king.

If you join his gym, you'd better be ready to work. The first week or two, the only thing Sonny will let you do is skip rope. Then, if he likes you, he'll let you start punching a bag. It takes at least a month before you do any sparring. Sonny's father was a boxer, and Sonny himself fought in the late 1940s, both as an amateur and a pro. His son and partner, Ernie, boxed in the early '70s. That's boxing family.

I am not into pain, but I am into drama and storytelling, and there's plenty of stories, both in and out of the ring. Each boxing match is a yarn that even the storyteller doesn't know the ending of: who will win and who will learn the lesson? And to each story comes a character with his own tale.

Being an arty lefty has thrown me in with groups of other peaceniks that sometimes make me feel even more alienated. A four-eyes such as myself often finds himself allied with special interests I don't quite agree with. I'm remembering the Gulf War protests of 1991, and how we all marched down Market Street, arms linked with socialists and queers and vegetarians and Goths and workers and animal rights groups, and before I knew it and against my will, the crowd was calling for a communist regime and an America that was meat, perfume, chemical, Republican, and army free. "All we are saying," we were saying, "is give peace a chance."

World peace. Singing in perfect harmony, all in agreement. The idea sends chills up my spine. Every day another mom-and-pop store is replaced by a chain. Soul food is replaced by fat-free cooking. Even churches have to be inoffensive—is there anything more dull and undramatic than the word "nondenominational"? When we talk about perfect harmony, we're talking about nothing less than the end of conflict, the end of plot, for Pete's sake. Secretly I do not want to give peace a chance. I prefer to give *War and Peace* a chance. I am not ready to give up fighting.

There are plenty of stories of conflict at M&M: Mike M., for instance, is a twenty-nine-year-old middleweight at 156 pounds. Originally from Denver, he now works at a photo lab after doing time in prison for drug dealing. Boxing has helped him focus on leading the straight and narrow life. When we talk, he's completely pumped about training for the upcoming Golden Gloves. "On the day I fight at the Cow Palace," he explains, "it will be one year to the day I was released from prison. I went to Golden Gloves eleven months ago and sat in the stands and I said to myself, I'm going to train and I'm going to be up there next year." And he will be. I ask him whether he did any boxing training in prison. "No," he smiles, "the only fighting there was unofficial."

The thing I hate most about pain is that most of it is invisible—unofficial. A boxer's job is to make his pain even less visible. To put it, as they say, in the closet.

Now that Larry Kramer has decided that Lincoln's first name was Gaybraham, the whole world, apparently, has gone gay. You might be expecting me to investigate the queer aspects of boxing. Okay, okay, here you go: guys jumping rope; guys in silk boxers; guys studying themselves in a mirror; guys giving other guys massages; guys meeting in a bed-shaped ring in their bathrobes, disrobing, hugging before they duke it out, dancing, coupling—well, uh-buh-*DUH*.

I suppose I'm not supposed to like boxing for all sorts of obscure reasons, like the fact that it was the Marquis of Queensberry who made up the Queensberry Rules and was also the man who triggered queer poster boy Oscar Wilde's infamous trials, and theoretically drove Wilde to his unhappy death. I suppose I shouldn't like it because big bullies have always beat up on big sissies.

But there is a connection for me more subtle than the guys-in-underwear thing, which has to do with what every sissy must learn: how to survive the tough world on sheer willpower. As one of the titular Viking Women of an old Roger Corman film once said, "We Vikings make our own fate!" If a fruit or a fighter wants to make it in this world, he must adopt that all-American battle cry.

Being a sissy, like being a boxer, takes sheer chutzpah. Don't mess with a seasoned queen, he's got his own version of a one-two punch. An adult sissy is one who survived years of torture (invisible pain) and is still alive. An adult sissy has learned he can't afford to lose.

A boxer always says he's going to win. Muhammad Ali said he was The Greatest. Mike Tyson said, "I try to catch my opponent on the tip of his nose because I try to punch the bone into his brain." This kind of swaggering is saddled with an odd-duck humility, one I see passed on from Sonny to his fighters.

Learning to be humbled by pain is an ongoing struggle. Nigel M., a Long Island native, is the super-heavyweight guy in training. He's a former football player who played for Boston University, then messed up his knee and was introduced to the wonderful world of painkillers. Addicted to them, he was led down the slippery slope of abuse. He didn't finish out that senior year in football and it took him years to get his life together. He and Mike work together at the photo lab, and the two of them went to watch the 1998 Golden Gloves together and decided to train for the next competition. Now Nigel is thirty-one and about to turn thirty-two, and fighting in this month's Golden Gloves will be his last chance—but he'll accomplish a personal goal. "It will be like finishing that last year of college football."

For Nigel, boxing turned out to be very different than he anticipated. He thought he'd be able to let his rage run rampant and feel a little power. The first thing Sonny made him do was drop seventy pounds. "I'm in a twelve-step program for overeating and it works for me the way it did for substance abuse," Nigel explains. "Twelve-step works for alcohol and drug abuse, but the problem is that when I'd get sober, I'd get angry. I thought I'd run the anger out at the fights, but it turns out that when you're mad, you completely lose form and discipline." There you have it: the most important thing to do while fighting is to control the anger while somebody is punching you. Nigel also found the "no talking in the ring" rule a challenge. "You'll get disqualified in a second," he says. Knowledgeably. And since there aren't that many super-heavyweights to fight with in Northern California, losing a fight on that kind of technicality can be very frustrating. Three of Nigel's fights have been called off on lack of opponents. Nigel is what they call a "green" super— and can only be matched with other green super-heavyweights. That's so he won't have the tip of his nose Tysonesquely punched into his brain.

"The best thing I've learned here," says Nigel, "is humility." Later he looks up at me thinking about the Golden Gloves and says, "I'm going to be so happy."

I recognize that happiness—a satisfaction at maintaining the uneasy confederation of hubris and humility. It's what marginal types create—people like my friend Hugh, for instance—and it's an uneasy union that artists and writers must forge within themselves. For an artist must be egotistical enough to believe she has something worth revealing to the world while also admitting that there is always more to reveal. Art is kind of like boxing. The savage beast within is tamed, the pain is squirreled away, the ego comes out in full force, the eyes are always looking for the ever-hidden victory.

🐾.

Eddie McCue has learned at an early age how to be an artist in the ring. He's a seventeen-year-old at Sacred Heart Academy, and was playing basketball until he got in a nasty fight with his coach, and that fight benched him. He told his dad, who grew up with Ernie Marson, that he'd like to take his hotheadedness into the boxing gym. He's been with Sonny for a year. "I'm starting to think in the ring." Eddie is excited. "There's a lot of strategy to learn. You've got to stay relaxed and calm. You can't be overaggressive." He's heading for San Francisco State next fall, and has a construction job on the side.

Then there's Jones Tom, who has a mother from Hong Kong and a father from mainland China, but he's a born and bred San Franciscan. Twenty-eight years old and 147 pounds, he also places in kickboxing state championships. He works security down at a pool hall, so don't let the middleweight build delude you. In sparring rounds, he holds his own against Leo from Galway, who is twice his weight. While all the other guys have a pro they admire—Eddie will study the moves of Hagler and Trinidad, Mike is a fan of Wayne "The Pocket Rocket" McAuliffe—Jones doesn't like to watch fights, he likes to *fight*.

And so Eddie from Sacred Heart is going at it with veteran Jones Tom. There are stains on the tarp of the ring, like a cheap hotel bedspread. Paris may have a point about the red-light district comparison. Both Eddie and Jones are wearing head guards, groin guards, and mouth guards. The rest is up for pummeling.

Both fighters match each jab with a gasp of breath that sounds a little like a MUNI train opening its doors. There's that rule in boxing again, the one where you can't talk to your opponent. Fights have ended because somebody was talking. I don't see how they can do it with those big purple retainers guarding their mouths.

The no-talking rule is curious. It's part of the "gentleman's sport" aspect of boxing, and contrasts nicely with the fact that all the guys I talked to at Sonny's gym were exceedingly articulate. And when they talked, they didn't complain; they enthused. But silence is golden in America; we value it in our streetwise heroes, everyone from Huck Finn to Clint Eastwood.

The boxing code of silence is different. For boxing is, if I am to interpret Paris Alexander's words about it being tough to find honest guys like Sonny in the boxing business, a pack of lies. "We fighters understand lies," said former champion José Torres. "What's a feint? What's a left hook off the jab? What's an opening? What's thinking one thing and doing another?" Maybe boxers keep their mouths shut in the ring in order to minimize the dishonesty.

What don't boxers lie about? Funny thing: their wins and losses. Paris told me he wins about half his fights. Winning doesn't seem to be the point. Since there's little money to be won in amateur boxing, the difference between winning and losing is pretty much the difference between eight bruises and nine. Success and failure aren't terribly different. I admire boxing because it seems to be an effort to redeem failure—and therefore pain. After all, you can still learn a lot from doing a geometry proof incorrectly.

All suited up now, Jones gives Eddie a drubbing, and when I watch Eddie I can see he knows the moves, the feints and shimmying. His shoulders and back are constantly rearranging themselves. I recognize the moves as stiff in the way learned things are stiff—no doubt soon enough they'll come natural to him, he'll style them for his own purposes. "Break!" yells Ernie when Eddie and Jones fall against each other. Eddie's got cuts under his eyes and after a second round, he gets a bloody nose, but they're absolutely normal. Sonny smears both their faces with Vaseline after each round, to minimize the breaks. There's blood on Eddie's T-shirt, and there's blood on Jones—but it's Eddie's blood. But Eddie has an edge: he's young.

"Young guys can heal faster," Paris Alexander explained to me. "They're also more optimistic. And they're too young to be odd." I figure "odd" means "nervous." Knowing when to quit is also a sticking point for these guys. "Sugar Ray Leonard retired four times," says Alexander. "When I retire, I'll do it once." Youth is as prized in boxing as it is by the culture at large. And yet the whole idea is to hide the youth, toughen it up.

·ᐤ·

That's why Paris Alexander, the pro, is in the ring with Eric Rios. Rios is the guy in this gym many of his fellow fighters are watching. He's almost eighteen and, originally raised under the volcano in Cuernavaca, he now goes to Balboa High School. Like Nigel, Sonny made Rios lose quite a few pounds since he started training in February 1997. Fifty pounds, to be exact. I'm thrown by his looks, for though he's Mexican, he has blond hair and wide Slavic cheekbones. He's already missing a front tooth, which I take to be a good sign. Sonny tells me that Eric wants to go to school to become a dentist.

In the sparring rounds, Paris is basically just bloodying the kid, toughening him with swat after swat. It's a peculiar kind of generosity, a selfish generosity, if you will; it's like how you're supposed to put your own oxygen mask on first before assisting small children if the cabin air pressure drops. But Paris's cat-and-mouse game is important and actually riveting. Alexander puts his mitts up in the air and creates an opening for Rios to punch at—and creates an opening on Rios for a pounding. That must be what they

mean by "sucker punch." But the next time Alexander creates an opening, Rios doesn't fall for it.

Boxers are bright. They're quick, both physically and
mentally. They have to be. If you ever saw the young
Muhammad Ali snap back with a couple of clever couplets
in taped live interviews, you know how impressive boxers
can be. There's a tradition of irony in boxing that you won't
find in some of the more dunderheaded sports: they call it
the "sweet sport"; they give themselves monikers like
Gentleman, Peerless, and Ruby. (Okay, I'm twisting the facts.
They also give themselves epithets like Assassin, Pocket
Rocket, and, my favorite, the inelegant and distracting Pride
of the Stockyards).

And if you think the ringside seats are filled with mob-
sters and molls, have you ever noticed that, unlike stadium
sports like NASCAR racing and football, even the most
drunken yahoo boxing fans never, *ever*, take off their shirts
at a boxing match?

Especially at Golden Gloves events. Golden Gloves is
amateur boxing—let's reclaim that word from its "unprofes-
sional" ties—amateur means "for the love of it," which is
what all these guys (and women, I'm told, but I see none at
M&M Boxing Gym) do. You must be between the ages of
seventeen and thirty-two to compete in Golden Gloves, and
you have to be registered. Dr. Ketchum, known fondly to the
boxers as The Fight Doctor, gives pro bono physicals to boxers. Sonny Marson takes good care of these guys. He's trying
to make a novice named Gordon quit smoking.

Marson is, of course, modest when I tell him I'm impressed with his operation. Well, modest to a point. There's a

precise amount of pride manifest in the two big gold rings, one on each hand, that remind me momentarily of the napkin rings I picked up at Pier 1 Imports. Other than that, he's salt of the earth. He and his girlfriend have a ranch somewhere out of town where he brings Title 90/20 kids for holidays to be in the country and get presents. This past Christmas, he hired green super-heavyweight Nigel to be Santa Claus.

He obviously cares deeply about boxing, but he also cares deeply about the boxers. Many of them are trying to get their lives back together after a stretch of trouble—prison, alcoholism, drug abuse. That may be one of the reasons Sonny is strict about diet. "Oh, that stuff will make you bleed," he said, "all that alcohol, sugar, salt." He puts them on milk.

Bleeding is a problem for boxers. Leo from Galway is a fine fighter and would be a major contender, but there have been times during a fight when they couldn't stop the bleeding and had to call the fight. The official rules in boxing say that you can't do anything about broken skin during a fight—you can only wipe a towel over it. Enter the "cut men," guys who have little tricks to stop the flow. There are some underhanded methods, guys who have adrenalin and other chemicals on their fingers. The same sorts of methods for keeping boxers from bleeding too much are used on roosters in cockfights. Men are not chickens, but it's hard not to think about the two events in a similar light. The way cocks are trained isn't that far off from the way boxers are trained, and the criteria for winning is not always winning, or staying alive, for that matter. Doing your best with what fate has dealt you, using your own strengths and weaknesses to their best advantage: good boxers see that in any fellow fighter. One good fight—the redemption of all the ordinary days that secretly deaden us.

One thing both women and men know is that it is more honorable to die passionately than it is to die in front of the television set. Defining the passion, that's the trick. So few people know what they want in life. This has always been surprising to me. These boxers know; Hugh knows. But most of us fumble around. Maybe bravery is also being unafraid to know what we want.

Sonny is a cut man, but his methods sound pretty holistic. "I got my training from a cut man named Enoch Yip," Sonny tells me. "He used to be the cut man for Ken Norton. He had these tricks he'd do with cotton yarn." I'm guessing there were herbal remedies involved, too, but those are ancient Chinese secrets Sonny wasn't ready to divulge.

Two more guys take to the ring. I'm feeling voyeuristic, like I've hung around this gym too long. Sure, real pain is invisible to others, but the fact is, people go to boxing in order to watch pain. Joe Frazier once said, "I don't want to knock my opponent out. I want to hit him, step away, and watch him hurt." I've said it before: there are very few times when it's culturally okay for one man to look at another the way he gazes at a woman. One is when a man is performing physical feats. Another is when he is sucking up pain.

I take another look over at Eddie, whose nose has stopped bleeding. Bleeding is an outward manifestation of pain. And yet bleeding is also the red badge of courage, maybe the closest approximation to the accurate gauging of pain.

Eddie sniffs a little, but it's just sucking it in, it's not crying or anything, and I wonder, maybe boxers feel pain differently, or there are certain kinds of pain that have redemptive qualities. After all, even I can recognize the kind of pain that can be—how to say it?—*worth* it.

Watching Eddie take his licks reminded me, selfishly, of my own personal battle. I was at the tail end of a painful breakup, and yet, while the hurt was excruciating, I would never have chosen not to experience it. I wanted it, even if it was going to run me into the ground. Cowgirl Jill reminded me that Cajun chef Paul Prudhomme loved rich food so much that he had to drink a glass of cream now and then, "just to refresh himself" between helpings. Now he walks with canes, when he's not on his motorized wheelchair. Sometimes what we love can defeat us. Eddie, in the ring, was duking it out for all of us.

The breakup, the relationship itself, did not make me necessarily happy, as Hugh would say. Knowing what you want, I thought, watching sweat and spit and blood aerosolize to the tune of golden oldies, does not lead to happiness, that old chestnut. But it is the binding force in me, challenges my own ability to rise to a moment—in the ring or at the crucial, defining, even fatal moment of one's life (I think religious people call this "grace")—and be who I am in spite of what this world expects me to be.

Hugh knows the worthwhile pain; it may not make him happy, necessarily, but pain does have replenishing powers. Pain is a fuel to help you be what you love. You know there is no hope of the conventional rewards the world typically bestows on conventional being, but that is not important. All these fights are their own rewards. Relationships can be that way, even when they fail. A fallen soufflé hails the advent of the next, flawless one. Even writing about boxing resembles the boxer's quest to turn pain into victory. A real victory may be as inscrutable and unmappable as pain, but it is always a victory of worthwhile pain.

# 6

# LAP DANCE

CAPTAIN ZAP ISN'T REALLY A CAPTAIN BUT A MAJOR IN the army, which is, I suppose, every queer boy's fantasy —somewhere between the rodeo and the boxing match, I found myself hanging out with an action figure. He teaches scuba diving and goes skydiving too. We're still planning on taking fencing classes. He even disciplined my ten-year-old dog to sit and not beg, which was the kind of revelation, as our friend Jill put it, that Helen Keller's parents must have experienced when the miracle worker proved she wasn't retarded and could indeed communicate with sign language.

Captain Zap was pleased to transport me and my educated grease-monkey friend Aaron to the Napa County Fairgrounds in Calistoga on a recent September evening for the annual World of Outlaws (that's "WoO" to you) Labor Day Harvest Classic sprint car racing.

What is WoO? Well, if Laguna Seca is at one end of the scale, a draw for the superrich, then consider World of Outlaws economy class. With any car-racing event, you can expect to find RV camping in the parking lot near the speedway. (It's a Brigadoon-like industry with shops and the usual suspects, like Schick razors, cheap beer, down vests,

T-shirts, and recreational vehicles on sale as well.) Think of the RV village as a kind of homing beacon—you never can get lost if you follow the churchy scent of citronella candles and dust.

It was a night of watching the dust settle, rise, then settle again near the moist Russian River, known in these parts as the Redneck Riviera. "Redneck" may mean working class (but let's put the emphasis on "working"—the red neck comes from hard labor under the sun), and "Riviera" means an expensive way to blow money.

Loving and blowing money is what keeps America together. These folks know how to do it because car racing, even the "Outlaw" kind, costs a lot of money. It's even more expensive if you're not just there to watch. To outfit a WoO car you've got to weld what's basically a backward-placed airplane wing on the top of your sprint car (it then performs the opposite of lift: it digs in) and install a superlightweight cage in the cockpit. There are other racecar accessories that cost money too, but I don't know what they are, because when Aaron told me the names of the costly parts, I realized that they baffled me the way I'm baffled when I hear teenagers enthuse over the latest cutting-edge band. In fact, there are auto-part terms that could be band names, and vice versa: "Whoa, dude, check out that Crank Case/Vapor Lock/Gearhead/Sludge Formation/V-Belt/Brake Drum!" The wrench-head society, for me, is another male secret elite society.

It's puzzling. Opera, one of my own personal weaknesses, has the immutable reputation of being the secret elite society sport of queens. It is said to require plenty of cash and intensive sartorial achievement, to be secretive to the point of freemasonry, to make grown men cry, and to kill with boredom. Car racing, to judge from the crowd at the race-way, is the wide-open sport of the masses.

Well, look here: Expensive? Dressy? Anybody—at least in San Francisco—can walk up the steps of the opera house, wearing practically anything (believe me, people do) and buy a standing room ticket for ten bucks. Meanwhile, the cheapest bleacher seats at World of Outlaws cost twenty-four stinkin' bucks! And the beers (piss! PISS! Hey, did I sound manly when I called the beer piss?) are four dollars a go-cup! You can get a friggin' tarte tatin at the opera for that much. Opera, like travel, will always be considered the lux-ury of a leisure class, because only the leisure class has time for a Wagner work or a trip to Europe. Team sports and car racing are strictly and puritanically timed—lollygagging is *soft*.

And opera is not so secretive. You can walk in cold and listen to an opera and know exactly what's going on when reading the supertitles, Meanwhile, the anonymity of those little helmeted heads encased in steel and rubber seems inscrutable to me. I'm sure Aaron and Zap could tell me who all those guys were, but even the most famous ones, when the helmet is off and they're endorsing Jiffy Lube or Taco Bell require identification on the screen: "This Is a Celebrity Endorsing Our Product."

Aaron explains a key difference in WoO cars: "It's a dry sump!", meaning there's no oil reservoir on the car. This is considered extraordinary, a manly miracle. But miracles, if you think about it, are really local and specific. If Moses had seen a refrigerator fall from the sky, would he have been as impressed as he was by a burning, blabbing bush? Not likely—a fridge would be too weird, and unprocessable by a Pentateuch prerefrigerant prophet. For all we know, God dropped dozens of home appliances on the Holy Land, but who could wrap their head around them? If you don't know the rules of a game, you don't know how amazing it is when the rules are broken. That's why a lot of car racing is totally lost on me.

And opera is boring? Okay, in matters of taste, there is no argument, but honestly, how long can you watch a car go around and around? In opera, somebody dies or goes insane, which is at least mildly interesting. I'd like to do a body count for a race season and an opera season. I know where I'd hedge my bets.

Actually I am sorry to point out that Kevin Gobrecht, a thirty-year-old WoO contender, who I watched win the First NAPA Auto Parts Heat Race (a contest with a name as clunky as a sprint car), 0.7 seconds ahead of Danny "The Dude" Lasoski, was killed in Greenwood, Nebraska, at the Cornhusker Outlaws Shootout (how could you not have violence with a name like that?), less than a month after I saw him.

What distinguishes World of Outlaws? It's "The Greatest Show on Dirt." They hose down a dirt track. But by the end of the night, during the final twenty-lap heat with as many cars, you wish they hadn't hosed it down, because hosing causes clumping, so instead of being covered in dust, you're pelted with pellets of compacted, dog-dirt-sized mud. Ouchy. I thought this was a spectator sport.

The cars look like some absurd end of a father-son soap box racer contest, and word has it, they have just about as much safety. They burrow at the air and dirt, determined as a doorstop, or that really short kid everybody called "Squirt" at school. And like the Squirt who was always picked on, WoO cars don't spar to play, they spar to survive.

There's plenty of danger to go around—you don't have to be a driver to get yourself obliterated. That's part of the fun, if I'm to read between the lines. Aaron, half disdainfully, half excitedly (I hope I'm writing this in the same spirit), tells me, "Oh, these things flip over when you breathe on them." Aaron's wife, Susan, has gone down on the track for a few races to wave the big checkered flag, and I dream of doing the same. If you squint your eyes and just wave the flag in front of you, you can pretend you are holding the similarly checked Maryland state flag and are proud to be from Baltimore.

Even behind a high chain-link fence (which does *nothing* to stop the kicked-up dirt clods), you are not safe. At a certain point in the evening—let us call it the highlight of the evening, unless you count the incident at the exit gates involving untended Schick razor giveaway boxes, and the subsequent pillaging and looting—a flaming tire detached itself from a passing car and leaped the fence, landing not six feet in front of us. WWMD? What would Moses do? The molten tire was immediately surrounded by six or seven scruffy white children.

Captain Zap pointed out, quite astutely, that all the children looked as if they were brothers and sisters, even though this shouldn't have been possible, since they were all about the same age. One of the children's parents screamed from behind our seats (and I am not lying or exaggerating, this was actually said): "Git aways from that tahr, Skeeter."

All the children backed up. Perhaps they were all named Skeeter. What is important to point out is that all the children came away unburned by the flaming tire. However, a full-grown adult, tall and pale and possibly a protector of children in a Boo Radley sort of way, reached down to the molten rubber and burned his hand. Hey, Boo.

Kids are often dragged to these events for whatever reason: lessons in teamwork, family togetherness, lack of a baby-sitter, Daddy said so. Kids only care about the carnage. At the bullfights in Valencia I sat behind a father-son bonding experience. The kid was filled with bloodlust—"*Mataló! Mataló!*" he'd hiss, and I'm not sure whether "Kill him! Kill him!" was goading the bull or the matador.

Are kids ready for these macho activities that have somehow evolved into family outings: bullfights, sprint car racing, wrestling, smash-up derby? Kids look at this stuff the way they'd look at any other kind of pornography, their imaginations at once wild and undeveloped. They focus on the hunt, not the kill, they leer at a flaming tire or a dead bull or matador the way we home in on the money shot in a skin flick. They don't understand that hurting hurts, they can't fully imagine what it is like to have a bashed-in skull or a sliced artery, nor can they fully appreciate what macho men know of aesthetics: the beauty of a well-oiled machine, the whole of an engine greater than the sum of its parts. If I had kids, I'd keep them away from this stuff, at least until they fell out of a tree and broke their arm and realize that the cat's head in a cartoon may get turned into the face of a frying pan when he gets hit in a cartoon, but turns into broken bone in real life.

I remember the definitive moment when I realized I was not immortal, and it was at another kind of car race. I was in sixth grade and trying to be cool by hanging out with three or four friends up at the high school where the older guys were drag racing their cars (the occasional Camaro and Z-28, but mostly Pontiac Astres and Bonneville Coupes). One of us small fry, my classmate David Henderson, was leaning against a car bumper when a Chevette pulled up fast, pinning him between the parked bumper and the newly arrived one. "Let me out, let me out!" he yelled angrily at the driver, and when the Chevette owner backed away a little, there was David. One leg fewer than the rest of us. To this day, I will not walk between two cars, parked or running. And it does not seem beside the point to inform you that the first thing David bought with the court settlement money he got for losing his leg was a zippy black Camaro, one with the gas pedal connected to the steering wheel.

So maybe I'm wrong to recommend that children not attend car races, because how are they going to learn?

And something else I understand: sometimes going to the races is the only way a loving wife can get in some quality time with her dude. I look into the crowd around me in the stands at the women—are they really watching, or are they, as women are so saintly good about doing, faking it? Some of them are genuinely into it.

I've decided that both Captain Zap and Aaron are what every wife—and some men—would want. While they never forget to have inner lives, they live pleasantly outside themselves, don't get worked up or panicky. They are handy. They are devoted. Smart yet not neurotic, they rise to the occasion. But make no mistake, we got lost on the way to Calistoga, and did we stop and ask for directions? No way. And by the way, Captain Zap has a Feminine Side. He's a Sister of Perpetual Indulgence (granted, his drag name is Sister Tipper Over, since she can't walk in high heels to save her miserable life) and (if this isn't macho, I don't know what is) has bicycled the entire California AIDS Ride from San Francisco to Los Angeles in nun drag. Captain Zap carried Aaron and me in a 4x4 usually cluttered with camping equipment and scuba gear—but he freaked Aaron out just a bit when he hauled into the fairgrounds a cooler full of . . . bric, pâté, little bitty toasts, and—*and*—a set of cute little knives with lambies and piggies for handles. Also, a couple of six packs. Six packs of Diet Pepsi. Oh. My. God. We are going to get *killed*.

I pop the top off a Diet Pepsi. With a wheel-about that can only be called Pavlovian, the guy in front of me, who looks like a member of ZZ Top thirty years from now, hollers, "Whatchoo smugglin' in here?" By this he means that we have all been searched at the gate for tools that undermine civilized life and the profit motive. These tools include knives, glass, guns, and your own beer. None of that fruity designer beer here, Buds. Besides, do you see a single car out on that track sponsored by St. Pauli Girl? The wife or girlfriend of the ZZ Top bearded guy (or groupie: the way she's applied her makeup, she might as well be loitering in a heavy metal concert parking lot) says, "Oh calm down, Porkchop, it's only a Diet Pepsi." Porkchop's T-shirt reads, "She won't mind getting a little dirty when you're sliding in the Big Johnson." What? I am sorry, but that requires operatic supertitles a lot more than Tosca's aria "Visi d'arte" does.

And by the way: *Porkchop*?

"Hey, Porkchop!" somebody yelled down to him. Then everybody hollered, "Hey, Porkchop." Everybody knew Porkchop. I offered him a Diet Pepsi, but he declined. Aaron, I noticed, moved two rows of bleachers behind us. That's when the flaming tire landed.

Car racing is surprisingly static, kind of like early opera, with lots of tableaux vivants and long periods of standing around. There's plenty of downtime between heats to check out the scene, in front of and behind the inconsequential chain-link fence. Each car has a major sponsor. Lots of them come from Pennsylvania, Hallowed Racecar Ground and the home of Pennzoil, Quaker State, and a host of racing royal families with distinguished names like Kinser, Unser, and Hillenburg. My favorite car is sponsored by Vivarin, the no-doze drug. Isn't that like showing plane crash films for the in-flight movie?

Do I like car racing? I don't want to say I don't, but I don't. Before you scorn me the way I scorn a movie reviewer who writes, "I don't like this kind of movie, so this movie sucked," let me explain. My interest is displaced, second-hand—but still as keen.

Other people's enthusiasms—especially for items I could care less about—are things I care deeply about. An ecstatic love for model trains, or gambling, or romance novels, or golf, or cars is at once boring and fascinating to me, like a glimpse at the inner motivations of a villain, or a lover. Personally I don't want to investigate those things in any depth, but when I meet people who do love them, I gravitate, I quiz, I want to know: why in the world? Any kind of enthusiasm, even enthusiasm for things that bore me, does not bore me at all. Passion is genuine, it lights us up with open egoless ecstasy, an endlessly attractive state.

Mostly men are shut down to hide their pleasures, because if somebody knows what you want, they might use it against you. It's a kind of combat technique, like in that apocryphal story about the medieval city held siege for over a month, and just when the invading army thought they had them and the people inside the walls were down to one last loaf of bread, the city's leader, rather than divide the bread among his troops, tossed the loaf over the city wall as if it were garbage. This, reportedly, caused the invading army to despair and give up the siege because obviously the inhabitants had bread enough to throw away. This lesson every man inherently understands, and hides his own loves in order to protect them.

But when that passion reveals itself, the soft, open surrender could also render an army unable to attack, because it is man at his most lovable. I am thinking here of a very particular situation in which Jeff, the electrician and carpenter guy I lived with until his death to AIDS, asked me in his healthier days to meet him for dinner at a pizzeria near his job site. I stood in front of the restaurant for fifteen, twenty, twenty-five minutes, then decided to walk to the house being built and hopefully find him en route. I walked all the way to the site exasperated and famished, but I was disarmed of all frustration when I saw him in an unfinished kitchen, sitting at the top of a folding ladder, holding an electric outlet and studying its various workings. His face was lost in love and interest for the lifework he had chosen, that egoless ecstasy. From that day on, I would ask him at bedtime to read out passages of the *Official Electrical Code Book for 1989*, and he had my rapt attention. Okay, that's an exaggeration, but you know what I mean.

Car racing, like electrical wiring, is a place where normally taciturn men become chatty, multisyllabic. The guys in the stands say things like, "It utilizes a 10.400 inch ceramic coated titanium rotor with a lightweight 200 series caliper." And then they start sticking decals all over everything, and building models, and getting all greasy and it's like they're twelve again.

Guys are lovable when they are truly, deeply in love with something or someone. Enthusiasm makes men brilliant and oddly soft, and men are usually enthusiastic about fast and shiny things. Aaron's into it. Captain Zap's into it. And hey—I can dig that.

Are we built for speed? Scientists say we'll all evolve into whimpy big-brained, long-fingered, delicate-eyed hairless aliens. I think it'll be just the opposite. We'll grow to withstand all the speed cars and roller coasters and extreme sports we put ourselves through, so our bodies will adapt into armored shells that can endure greater speed and impact. We'll get a sort of pleasure from crashing, the way we get high from little amounts of poison in alcohol and tobacco and coffee. But under the armor, we'll stay soft and vulnerable like boys, like one-legged David Henderson, just like we've always been. I like boys. Do girls like boys in the same way? Maybe they're not faking it there in the stands either.

It's only around the hardest surfaces (the spikiest, the hottest, the toothiest) that men's softness finally comes into vivid relief. They cannot be silent: I see those frozen-faced mountaineers on top of Everest, oxygen deprived, babbling. They cannot look like they do not care: I see Jeff drink in every page of the *Electrical Code* with those soft brown eyes. And they cannot be unbreakable: I see David Henderson, like it was yesterday, leaning against his flashy sleek black metal B-2 Bomber of a Camaro, propped on one foot, and with one pointless trouser leg folded up and over itself several times, pinned in place as neatly as an American flag, retired from the pole for the night.

# 7

# THE INCREDIBLE SHRINKING MEN

HE'S PICKING UP TRASH ON THE SIDE OF THE FREEWAY, sweating like a pig, inhaling car exhaust as drivers zoom past. Once in a while, a flap of his fluorescent orange visibility vest blows open when a semi barrels through, and you can read his T-shirt: "Actually, I'm Going to Be a Director."

We're all going to quit our day jobs, anytime now. We're going to be directors or actresses or painters or screenwriters. Or maybe not. Maybe we're going to win the lottery. Maybe we're going to fall in love and get married and have a baby and stay home and raise a family. Maybe an executive headhunter will call and give us that dream career.

Whatever it is, a year from now, we're not going to be cleaning up trash alongside the freeway. But in the meantime, we won't complain that we're being paid eight dollars an hour to ruin our eyesight at a computer terminal, or that we're begging for tips after slinging twenty lattes a minute. Above all, we're not going to complain that we are wearing the silliest damn outfit that has ever been called a uniform—brown, double-knit polyester, complete with doofy tall hat and pants with a plastic zipper. To fight for workers' rights (or even workers' dignity) would suggest there's a remote possibility we'll be in these ridiculous things for more than the next six months. Which, of course, we won't.

Perhaps this reluctance to acknowledge the way we make our living explains the ongoing use of such things as the Hot Dog on a Stick ensemble (employees work in these wiener-shaped franchise stands wearing polyester mustard brown on polyester mustard yellow, with matching top hat), uniforms that are silly without redemption (as opposed to the navy sailor uniform, which is silly *with* redemption: those bell-bottoms that may, in the distant past, have served some function still show off sailor butts very nicely, and that's function enough).

Marching-band uniforms are a classic case of items of clothing no longer functioning as they were intended. Dark capes with bright inner linings are not made to keep band members warm during chilly October football games, but to flash dramatically during a quick about-face while they're high-stepping across the field. Similarly the spats that were originally created to keep rain and mud from slithering into a man's shoes remain in use only in marching uniforms to get that flash of white as the foot comes up. Tragically the modern spat does just the opposite of what its predecessor was designed to do: marching-band spats are highly effective in funneling water and mud into the shoe, which explains why many of the musicians have chronic colds through the autumn months. I know about this because I was a big marching-band geek, all the way through college. The uniform, the drilling, the anonymity appealed to me.

♨.

When I start flipping through my high school yearbook, whose cheap glue still smells like puke the way all institutional things do, it doesn't look so awful. Group shots make everybody look harmonious. Marching-band uniforms go a long way to ensure that.

There is only one picture of me in which I'm not indistinct, the mug shot. I'm shiny and look embarrassedly red; I'd just started shaving and acne forced me to use whatever astringents I could get, most of which only angered the pimples. I recall pulling from my face the thready traces of cotton balls that had snagged on whiskers.

There is only one picture of me, although on another page is a picture of a bunch of bare feet running around under a big Chinese dragon. The feet up front are mine. There I am, the incredible shrinking man.

That was my favorite horror movie, a lackluster preference in a golden age of scarier, gorier films full of mutant babies, aliens, and sharks. But *The Incredible Shrinking Man* somehow stuck. I could relate. Vacationing in a pleasure boat, our hero makes his wife go down into the galley to get him a beer, and he is punished for mistreating her by being exposed to an eerie radioactive mist, which causes him, over the course of a year, to get smaller and smaller, until he fights a cat from his dollhouse and then, well, disappears.

Initially I related to him because in our town there was no such thing as a junior high school, and in seventh grade, we were thrown in with the big kids. If we were not locked into broom closets, snapped with jockstraps, or given flat tires in the halls, we were tiny, undeveloped, under the level of the horizon. Shrimps.

*The Incredible Shrinking Man* also resonated to me because maybe I envied him, while also fearing his fate. As a gay boy, I was not the nelliest. I avoided the nelly ones, it's true. I could, as transvestites say, "pass." Unlike Eugene

Smith, who was doomed with his sensitive white skin and slender, damnedly graceful long limbs (and Lordy, he chose to play the *flute* in band), and Steven Shippe, who was foolhardy enough to give Mr. Barrett, the athletic director, a note that actually read, I kid you not, "Please excuse Steven from showering after physical education class because Steven does not sweat. Signed, Mrs. Mary Shippe."

I was bad at sports, but it was chalked up to clumsiness. Lazy eye, unchecked, gave me permanently bad motor skills; to this day I must budget for broken wine glasses and stained ties. I played French horn in band, which is bulky and brassy enough to not appear phallic and fussy as long as you didn't look too closely at the prissy, pursy mouthpiece. Besides, Greg Watts was first chair and I was second, and he was known to get in fights regularly and was excused from marching band in the fall to run cross-country, a lonely but not faggy sport.

I hoped that in clumsy ordinariness, I could seem invisible. The problem was, I was kidding myself. It has to do with breeding. Vendekemp Lake is a tiny corner of Michigan. I was of distinguished stock there. My grandparents had gone to the school with the same name, and my parents had gone to the same building that I did, wandered the same halls, exactly. In all the history of histories of Vendekemp Lake, my father was the most famous and talented athlete the school has ever produced: quarterback, shortstop, basketball all-star. They even let him play two sports in a single season because they needed him to pole vault the track team to victory. And my mother was the prettiest, most popular cheerleader in the history of popular cheerleaders, homecoming queen, Daughter of the American Revolution.

My father was a manly man, and a nice guy too. He brought the Jayhawks to state championships in both football and basketball. He was an Eagle Scout and a member of the Key Club, whatever the hell that was. My brothers live there and their children now go to the school.

Things do not change much in Vendekemp Lake, and if they do, there's a fuss. A shopkeeper moves the freezer section to the back of the store and there are letters to The Voice of the People in the *Citizen-Patriot*. The reversion of a two-way street to One Way means war. And so for me, the oldest of my father's three sons, to enter the school and to wish only to be invisible—not popular, not athletic—this was not acceptable.

Not acceptable to whom? When Steven Shippe handed his arid letter written by his overmothering mother to Mr. Barrett, the athletic director, what do you think happened? How do you think the athletic director, a man who had coached my father and still lived on Brylcreem and American Hoo-Ha and took a beehived wife just a few years older than my mother right out of Vendekemp Lake High School, handled that little note?

Was Mr. Barrett a discreet man who knew that if such a note was made public, Steven Shippe was worse than dead? Did he do the intelligent thing and call Steven's hand-wringing mother and explain that this was no solution? Did he do the adult thing and discuss it with other school officials? Did he even do the manly thing and ignore it? No. He did the lousy thing, and when we were all lined up in our roll-call squads, he read the letter aloud to us.

Let me give Mr. Barrett a little credit: he sped things up. Steven Shippe's doom was only hastened along, for it was inevitable: he would either be parboiled slowly and have his skin flayed over a long time, or be crisped in Mr. Barrett's deep fryer of manly disdain. Mr. Barrett, despite everything, could tell right away who did and did not fit in. Soon after, Steven became part of some experiment in homeschooling or distance learning. And I got the message loud and clear: do not stand out. Get invisible. Uniforms could do that. I joined marching band, I joined Boy Scouts, I even stepped into the divine cassock of the altar boys. Shrink, shrink, damn you.

But now I'm all grown up, and I've learned that uniforms may also be used to stand out, rather than blend in. They're leisure wear, not work wear. I'd heard about the Premier Mr. International Rubber competition, held in November in Chicago, the week before when I told my friend Ed that I'd soon be paying him a visit. Ed and I had carried on a long-distance relationship when we were in college. I went to school in Chicago, he in Colorado. Once, in a premonition of things to come, Ed had decided to surprise me by arriving at my door in a leather harness hidden under his clothes. He'd forgotten about the metal detectors at the airport, and when he set them off, he was subjected to a full, humiliating search.

Perhaps not so humiliating—thirteen years later, Ed's partner, Ash, a wry EPA lawyer, can only smile lovingly when Ed shows me his latest achievement—he's made the cover of *Bound and Gagged*, dressed in a cop's uniform and trussed up in "Police Line Do Not Cross" tape.

"This weekend is Mr. International Rubber," he said. "Are we going?"

Ed's offer to guide me through the Inferno that is Chicago's S&M scene, the headquarters of International Mr. Leather, was hard to refuse. I could investigate those dank, beery oubliettes like the cooped-up Cell Block, the dimly lit

Hoist, the unsavorily named Manhole, and the incvitable Eagle with a friend to show me the ropes and make sure that if someone put a bottle of poppers under my nose I wouldn't disappear into some chain-filled dungeon never to return.

"There's a dress code," Ed warned. A *uniform*.

No problem. In his lovely home, Ed leads me downstairs past the jars of canned tomatoes and recycled newspapers into his basement dungeon with a big steel locker full of uniforms: football players, Marines, night guards, cops. Chaps, jocks, boots, jerseys, and some chain-mail thing he must've jousted off King Arthur. "This is where the sling goes," Ed points up to four strategically placed eyelets, "but I think I'm going to move it over here." "Here" is a place a little further away from the washer and dryer.

Ed is generous. He gives me jeans, chaps, and a blue T-shirt that reads "Chicago Police," an item that gets me many admiring slaps and compliments throughout the evening. He gives me a leather jacket and big fat rubber yellow-banded fireman's boots.

Ed wears his latex tank top and chaps. "The best thing about rubber is that it doesn't just come in black. You can get it in red, yellow, or white." Ash comes down to do a load of brights and watch us dress. He's not joining us, but he is concerned and a little curious: "Is it okay to wear white latex after Labor Day?"

We take the Beemer to the Cell Block. Inside, things are warming up. The show starts at 8:30, early for leather and rubber men. There are some fine latex outfits milling around. There's a guy in a Scout uniform with a latex kilt, and I feel the twinge of recognition. There's a man wandering around looking like a male Catwoman with a full mask; the stretchiness of the stuff makes the holes for his eyes and mouth pinch, so he looks like he's pursing his lips the whole night. Another guy has so many buckles and straps he looks like a piece of luggage. The bouncer by the back room, a bleach blond who shockingly is not a contestant, has latex chaps and a studded jockstrap. "Isn't that painful?" I ask Ed.

"It's *about* pain, dummy," he drawls.

We are at the climax of what they're calling Rubber BlowOut Weekend, and I'm sorry to have missed the Friday night cocktail reception, the rubber fetish party, the morning brunch, the rubber swap meet, and the too-rich-for-my-blood Dungeon Play Party (thirty bucks, please). On Sunday there's the Rubber Ball (boing), and Ed intends to enter what he thinks might be the Mr. Rubber rival group's competition. Yikes, is there a Rubber Schism?

Nah. There's plenty of camaraderie; one of the judges for our contest is Mr. Vulcan Rubber 1997, the velvety Rich Villagracia. Live long and prosper, Mr. Vulcan!

Our MC is a giant man named Kris Francis. Kris has a handful of canned jokes, but he's also quick on his feet, a raunchy Don Rickles act leavened with self-effacing obesity quips. Ultimately he's the reason to pay for this party (ten dollars at the door, five returned to you in funny money redeemable at the bar).

♪.

In Europe, where folks are much more fatalistic about work, uniforms are nicer and have become both comfortable and attractive, not to mention functional. Paris street cleaners wear zippy chartreuse ensembles and sweep the roads with brooms made to look like bundles of twigs bound together, even though they're completely made of plastic. The arborists in the parks of Barcelona look sharp in bright green coveralls. It was a delicious sight, while walking in rainy Galicia, to see rows of blue coveralls drying a shade lighter, like paint, on the clothesline.

Down south, in Mexico City, every profession has a uniform. The woman at customs stamps passports in a midnight blue jacket, and she even wears an inscrutable uniform expression, her face like a Mayan ruin. On the subway, you may encounter a man in a military-like uniform with an elaborate armpatch, a lightning bolt splitting a circle emblazoned with the words *Luz y Fuerza* ("Light and Power"). It makes you wonder: Is he part of an elite army strike force? Is he a religious fanatic? Or does he work for the electric company?

Uniforms serve both to clarify and to make ambiguous. By exhibiting what you do through what you wear, you make your function in the workday world easily identifiable, but that also makes it harder for people to recognize you as an individual. How much do you want to be recognized as an individual on the job? How much do your employers want you to be recognized as an individual?

My mail carrier is a groover dude, and apparently he's only required to wear one piece of the uniform as he saunters door to door. He chooses the shorts, gray with a blue stripe down the sides. They're adorned with a long chain from which hangs his wallet. He wears V-necked T-shirts and Nikes. I don't mind much.

But we depend on uniforms for their recognition factor, for narrowing the playing field: a guy wearing a ten-gallon hat and chaps is either a cowboy or a leather queen; a woman with one of those short-on-the-top-long-in-the-back haircuts (a hairdo known as the "shlong" or "S&L Crisis") is either a rocker chick or a FedEx carrier. That sounds prejudicial, but people within subcultures *want* signifiers. They cut to the chase.

Uniforms at work also bring us quickly into the place we want to belong. Businessmen hitch up their silk ties, no longer functional. (Oh, but think about the subtleties of that workplace fashion statement, how only boldly striped silk and wide with a tight knot at the neck will do, how foolish the flat-bottomed double-knit type looks, how the dorky retro-new-wave skinny tie is right out.) Many a union laborer will tell you hard hats are often more symbolic than necessary.

Uniforms create power when seen in numbers—they symbolize a united front, an e pluribus unum that makes a man both invisible and hard to miss. And that's just where most guys like to be.

♣.

Teachers, beware your students: they are your future biographers. Mr. Chuck Barrett, gym teacher: the Story of the Mandarin Emperor comes to mind, the one who presided over a town of great tranquillity. When a visiting official from the capital came to the town to marvel at the prosperity of the emperor's province, he explained how he maintained such order and peace by drawing his sword and, at chest level, running it over a field of grain in a radius around his body. Any of the wheat stalks growing higher than his chest were snicked off, until all of the wheat was exactly the same height. There's another thing uniforms, uniforming, does.

Mr. Chuck Barrett had a sword, and quite a chest.

My mother had taken me to the high school in our Vista Cruiser station wagon to register in late August the year before, when I first entered this school. I remember an odd expression she got, as if she were fighting back tears. She said to me, "These are going to be the happiest years of your life."

Two years in, the thought that I was peaking here, that my time with these people would be the best, that it got no better—this made me feel like an alien, like the incredible shrinking man.

Scott Carey was the name of the Incredible Shrinking Man. As he got smaller, his sweet wife made him smaller and smaller clothes, and the doctors tried to find some antidote in a race against time. As he shrinks, he becomes more alone (and, at the risk of drawing attention away from this existential point, he also becomes more naked and sexy). Eventually he has to live in a dollhouse, do battle with the pet cat, eat moldy cheese from a mousetrap, and (in a loincloth) fight to the death with a spider. The ordinary world to Scott Carey is nothing but danger and challenge. The only thing that keeps him going for a while is writing his feelings in a journal. The horror of his situation is subtle, for what is the inevitable outcome of this shrinkage? Disappearing, zero, nothingness.

The Incredible Shrinking Man both terrified me and thrilled me. I recognized too well the fears he had, and I looked for his rewards. Going on, intact, seemed the one satisfaction in life as I was thrust into an alien landscape where what came simply to others—splitting up into a boys' wall and a girls' wall at a dance, the firm belief that *Happy Days* was a program far superior to *Laverne and Shirley*, the sudden uncoolness of enthusiasm—ensnarled me. The ban on enthusiasm was strictly reinforced by the teachers in the reign of Mr. Barrett. It was another way to snick off the higher wheat stalks.

Extra energy, enthusiasm—these were only allowed to be vented in phys ed. Just as my mother, full throated, assured me that these were the best years of my life, The

Emperor Barrett began the school year by dividing us into squads and announcing that this, undoubtedly, would be the funnest class of the day.

What fun! To have a jokester like Joe Weaver slip up behind you and shuck your gym shorts down to your ankles so that the girls, on their side of the gym, might observe the fit and cut of your jockstrap. To be spanked with a pornographically large paddle riddled with holes, just for leaning against the rolled-up wrestling mats. The swirlies, the towel snapping.

The Emperor Barrett, what was he like? A Ronald Reagan without the wit. He pronounced "nuclear" "nucular" and "poem" "poim." Studying his picture in my yearbook, I can see that he was exceedingly fit for a man in his late fifties and his face did not wrinkle so much as crease, which must have made shaving difficult. Brylcreem, yes, but something else in his hair, too, like boot polish. The requisite whistle and ubiquitous clipboard, the form-fitting short-sleeved double-knit shirt, an unembarrassed comfortableness in pleated shorts; a model of nonenthusiasm for us all to copy, a face impassive, a rare smile meant only for mocking, a phrase or two, Spartan, that praised or damned or both.

I couldn't hide from him. The Incredible Shrinking Man was under the microscope. He knew and hailed my father and his father; his wife was my mother's classmate, they cheered together. I was to be the golden progeny of that golden age now gone, for fifteen years had passed and Vendekemp Lake Jayhawks had not taken any more championships, nor even attended playoffs. In the cafeteria there was a massive stand of sports photographs of the greats. It was all about my father. In the trophy case near the principal's office was a photograph yellowed into oblivion of my father on one knee, fully uniformed, his helmet in his hand like the skull of some great enemy, conquered.

The Emperor Barrett was not surprised by my lack of athletic prowess. Rumors had bubbled up even from Little League baseball, when I played for three years for a team sponsored by Vandy Party Store (purveyors of beer kegs, pickled eggs, and Pop Rocks) and roamed the quiet outfield like Lucy Van Pelt. Season after season I was promised the largest banana split if I'd just hit a home run—okay, a base hit—okay, a bunt—okay, just a foul ball, for Christ's sake. The uniform, emblazoned with our sponsor, did nothing to help me blend in out there either.

I attended required physical education classes on the eve of a new era, when the state mandated integrated boys' and girls' sports. If a two-way street turned One Way meant war, coed sports was holocaust. The Emperor Barrett, athletic director, was very slow to comply. It wasn't until the spring of tenth grade that he grudgingly allowed us to play volleyball for three weeks with the girls. He mocked silly games that accommodated girls: square dancing, softball, archery, bowling.

Enthusiasm volcanoed out in gym class. Doug Priest threw a stray cat against a wall as hard as he could out by the field house, to the Emperor Barrett's delight. I recall Joe Blankenship falling from roughly two stories up on the rope, and being told to quit crying you big baby, and his returning to school with a strap to hold his broken collar bone in place. I did my best to keep a low profile, but the Emperor Barrett would not allow this.

"How about Bouldrey?" he'd shout when team captains picked sides and the choice players dwindled. "Doesn't anybody want Bouldrey? He's an *asset.*" He hauled back with the medicine ball a little harder with me. I was a thorn in his side.

"Run, Bouldrey, run," he charged on the fifty-lap day. I am the long-distance runner. I run at a blend-in pace, but I keep running. I persevere, and while even track stars tuckered out on forty laps, I stomped away and passed them all. As I finished the last five laps with a clear lead, attention on me for the first time, oxygen-deprived, I fantasized about a new era: a cross-country champ. My lungs grated away, my upper body went to sleep as I finished big—and collapsed in a ball of exhaustion on my knees at The Emperor's feet. It felt like there was driveway gravel in my throat. His lips drew back into some kind of smile, the way a donkey makes to bray, or a chimpanzee to mug. He would congratulate me, though, I thought. He would see my undiscovered potential. He would bring me into the elect, the ones he let sit on his desk after school and hang out.

When the Incredible Shrinking Man was flooded out of his matchbox by the hot water heater, hanging onto a pencil for dear life, he was sure his wife would hear him call for help and save him. But he'd shrunk too small, his voice was too tiny. The Emperor Barrett looked down at me wheezing for air and he said, "I bet your mommy didn't know you could run that fast."

Enthusiasm deferred ekes out eventually. You can see it in elaborate baroque churches built in Spain at the height of the repressive Inquisition. It squirts out like toothpaste in the Manolino architecture of phlegmatic Portugal, and the Olympic zeal of the Soviets and pushy, rococo gangsta rap and Eskimo blanket tosses and Peking opera and English Morris Dancing. It's striking and revealing.

I revealed my enthusiasm in the gym that day, my biggest mistake. It was a lesson that I have never forgotten for, as I said, the Emperor Barrett sped things up. Never let them know what you want: it's like the message of a Russian poem.

·ℒ

At the Mr. International Rubber competition, the contestants hit the stage one by one. There are only five, and I'm not sure whether that's because nobody knew they had to sign up in advance or because they've already narrowed the field to this handful. The rules are straightforward: all competitors must own their own rubber, they may not bribe the judges, they may not expose the family jewels.

The first contestant, a leggy, grinning guy, comes out wearing a rubbery short-sleeved shirt and shorts of black and red. He is followed by ein Hamburger, dressed like one of Jacques Cousteau's crew sans flippers. His English is limited to "I like to be a bottom and bark like a dog." He demonstrates for us. Number three is Walt, a compact wrestler wrapped in a singlet. Fourth is the latex antihero, a dumpy fortyish guy in a "Daddy's Boy" baseball cap. He's got a gut and resembles, vaguely, one of Dr. Seuss's Sneeches. No stars upon thars, unfortunately, but he did make his own latex outfit, painting rubber goop on a jockstrap and a pair of sandals, which are all he's wearing. The final contestant is Christoph, who teaches philosophy for a living. That is so hot. He's wearing a stylized latex thong and thigh-high hip boots. The contestants take a bow and file off stage to await the second portion of the competition.

During the intermission, I find that the imperious uniform look of men into S&M is often undermined by their conversations. When I roam around the bar, I overhear exchanges about home decorating and real estate. I imagine a nation of Eds, the sling next to the ironing board.

Passing the time in the prescribed method, Ed and I watch a video screen showing ghastly solo porno of a man in a rubber suit. There's an elaborate gas mask over his face; it's like a scene from David Lynch's *Dune* left on the cutting-room floor.

"What's it about?" I ask Ed. Not just the aesthetic, but the pleasure principle.

"Control," Ed says. "Controlled breathing, in the case of the gas mask. Lots of these guys like to choke themselves during sex, because it heightens the orgasm." It's also about cash. This stuff is not cheap. No wonder so many guys are talking about real estate and decorating: by day, they're executives and lawyers, stuffing their alter egos into a closet full of pricey latex. And for all of its tough-guy aura, latex can be punctured by a careless fingernail, so hands off the merchandise, mister, unless you really mean it.

I eavesdrop on a conversation between a guy in a leather jacket and an edible-looking, candy-apple-red latex tie and a rubber salesman. He's telling the rubber salesman that he's designed a line of latex cowboy shirts, complete with yoke and fringe. A beefy dude in latex shorts so tight he looks like a wrapped ham is trying to rustle up enthusiasm for the Camp Mud outing, a messy weekend of rassling in filth held each August on a ninety-acre Wisconsin farm.

Part two of the competition is a question-and-answer portion. MC Kris has contestant number five bend over in his shiny rubber thong. "Come into the light, Carol Ann!" he commands. The question: What is the first piece of rubber you ever bought, and why? The answers are lackluster—shirt, shorts, boots; but then, I'm hoping for more baroque answers—gardening aprons, maids' uniforms, fedoras, a marching-band uniform, please.

The Rubber Fantasy competition follows. What do you dream of doing in rubber? Our Hamburger informs us, "I like to be a bottom and bark like a dog." There are locker room, nude camping, and gang-bang scenarios. These do not seem fully realized, and they don't even come close to breaking the rules: "Your fantasy must be within City of Chicago statutes, which means no exposure of genitals. . . . City of Chicago building codes must also be observed." Building codes?

Our contestants roam the audience and "cruise," a kind of squeaky lap dancing parade by way of segue into the next segment: the Erotic Buff Job. All five contestants take a spray bottle and a cloth to each other, shining up the latex to a high gloss. There really is a transformation—suddenly, what might have passed earlier as recycled bike inner tubes sports a finish that dazzles, and even the Sneech is able to coax a bit of spiffiness out of his homemade outfit.

Things are really just getting started, but already it's time to announce the winner. The Sneech, sadly, didn't place (I voted for him because he was not nearly as conspicuous a consumer as the others), nor, surprisingly, did the grinning guy. Third place goes to the Hamburg Barker, second to compact singleted Walt. My philosophy professor takes the gold appropriately, graciously. He dons the medallion and takes a Miss America tour of the room, holding his trophy for the cameras. The Easter basket of Wet Lube products is his, as well as $750 cash—not too shabby for a night spent traipsing around in a pair of flyfisher's wading boots.

The crowd is jubilant, and the night is young. I check my watch: midnight, and the crowds are starting to pour in. Jeez, I'm usually in bed at this hour, reading a book. It's smoky and hot and I'm way behind in the piercing-and-tattoo department. I yawn meaningfully at Ed. There's a midget lesbian bound to the chain spiderweb in the back, so he's willing to call it a night.

♫.

There was one other place enthusiasm could be vented during high school: in a disguise. Costumes, including uniforms, offered a Mardi Gras escape. There was an anomalous teacher, clearly gay, who was accepted without discussion. I think there's one in every town, the queen who is tolerated because somebody is needed to direct the town theatricals.

His name was Mr. Hodges, and he was tremendously hairy except for the top of his head. Barrel-chested and sartorially achieved, he talked with an inscrutable Southern lilt, a little sandy, bourbony, like he'd been watching documentaries about Tennessee Williams and Truman Capote rather than actually living in the South. Not even the toughest bully ever said anything about his soft-spoken, hall-monitor remonstrances, ubiquitous cans of Diet Pepsi, or impeccable pastel outfits. It was as if he were one of those tiny pink fish, vulnerable snack food to every finned predator, that is somehow able to live, impossibly yet comfortably, among the poisonous tentacles of a man-of-war.

Why was he allowed to live? For the sake of art. Mr. Hodges made his name household when he presented a production of Gilbert and Sullivan's *The Mikado* all done in blue and white, the set exactly reproducing the design of willow-pattern china. Sheer genius. He also directed the annual Junior Miss pageants. But his finest hour was an annual homecoming coronation of king and queen.

While most schools marched the candidates for this honor out onto the football field at halftime for a perfunctory ceremony, most of the king candidates still in uniforms

THE INCREDIBLE SHRINKING MEN | 97

and helmets, the girls looking silly next to them on the fifty-yard line in an evening gown, Mr. Hodges gave the crowning great dignity.

After the game, win or lose, everybody filed into the gymnasium and sat on bleachers. Depending on the theme of the homecoming parade—Let's Go to the Movies, Disneyland, Space the Final Frontier—the pageant that evening followed suit. One year the theme was It's a Small World, and each of the queen candidates sat on a small throne on a platform on wheels, four of them decorated as if they were from a different country: Italy with a cardboard cutout of the leaning tower of Pisa, England with Big Ben. Each one of these dollies had to be pushed from behind by a boy so that the audience could see the candidate do a circuit, wave like a princess, and be transported to the main stage where the final crowning would take place. Mr. Hodges asked me to push Natalie Gutchess, a pretty senior who didn't know I was alive, thank God. She was put on the France float, with an Eiffel tower. I had to wear a little beret but was blissfully blocked by the huge tricolor.

Even the Emperor Barrett must have approved of all this stuff, since it was really all about football and most of the king candidates were his boys. And while Mr. Hodges swished through the preparations, not even the Emperor could imagine him being sexual; besides, he kept cigars too, which created a manly smoke screen. In the years after I left the school, my younger brother, who was athletic and well loved, was crowned homecoming king after the big game, shouldered with a golden robe and a manly crown. Who pushed my brother's queen around on a dolly, who was the incredible shrinking man four years after me?

The pommerrettes performed with flashlights to "It's a Small World," and most elaborate of all, Mr. Hodges had built a big Chinese dragon, and six of us were to roll up our pant legs, climb inside, and race around to frantic oriental xylophone music. I was asked to control the big papier-mâché head, and, without practicing, instructed to shoot the nozzle of a fire extinguisher through the mouth to make the dragon breathe fire.

"Serpentine, serpentine!" he shouted to our little team of barefoot coolies, meaning we needed to look longer, and wilder. As I sprayed the contents of the extinguisher out, it landed on our feet, and they were nearly lost to frostbite.

There are only two pictures of me in the yearbook that year: my mug shot in the class photo section, and my bare feet at the front of the dragon at homecoming. I was comfortable in that papier-mâché head, cold feet or no, fantasizing that maybe I really was far away, in China. If I could have spent my entire high school career with just my feet showing, it would have been perfectly perfect.

Did I discover the criteria for perfectly perfect in the world of latex? The judges were asked to consider creativity, content, and audience appeal. But what touched me was the fetishists' goofy sweetness. This is a world full of Sneeches and philosophy profs with as many fantasies about buying real estate as getting laid. In a world where the sling hangs next to the washer and dryer, and white (yes, even in latex) is inappropriate after Labor Day, perhaps what's truly excellent about the Rubber World is the way fantasy can coexist so peaceably with reality.

I went to Amsterdam the following year with Captain Zap. Amsterdam is the city where they've become rational about the irrational. Desire is not going away, so why not plan for it? Since Zap made a career in the army, he knows the allure of uniforms, how they help erase the line between work and pleasure, how they simultaneously make you invisible and visible. It should be no surprise that Zap wanted to buy some latex while we were in a town where the *oudest kerke* is surrounded by prostitutes in fantasy boudoirs come-hithering through plate-glass windows.

"Black Body" was like a chamber of horrors, only a *boutique* chamber of horrors, long and narrow and lined with gas masks and eyeless masks that, when unzipped, revealed another mask, blooming like a nightmare tulip. Latex pants, latex restraints, latex codpieces—Captain Zap started loading up his arms with pricey outfits to try on in the dressing room. The proprietor, in a latex jacket and tank top, asked me, "Would you like an espresso?"

I would be delighted, I said, and sipped from my demitasse as Zap came out in outfit after outfit and I approved and disapproved—nope, that one makes your legs look skinny; nope, that one plunges too low; yes, that one really shows off your stuff.

Zap had to buy the special polish too, and talc, and a polishing cloth—the expense of latex is only surpassed by its delicate quality. And yet it's directly tied to toughness, macho, and the ultimate games of pain and control. These days the uniform that has succumbed to fashion is a thing requiring hard work to maintain, rather than accommodating hard work. Captain Zap now has an outfit that can make him blend in among the manly gay men of the Eagle/Hoist/Powerhouse, but out on the street, there's nowhere to hide.

In the winter of my Year of the Dragon, a strange event occurred. It had to do with a quiet guy named Francis Bausch, fairly good at all the sports and, in retrospect, hard to peg as a *type*. He was from a poorer family and hung with roughnecks and had a knack for fixing cars and lawn mowers; he was never mean to me, but then we shared hardly any classes together. Already we were sold down the river of capability, he on the course toward vocational technology, I toward college prep. But gym period is the time and place where all classes meet, the smart, the stupid, the skilled, the clumsy, the good, the bad, the ugly. This was phys ed's simultaneous punishment and reward: it was the great leveler, like the white uniforms of pilgrims to Mecca that render rich and poor indistinguishable.

Francis and Joe Blankenship—the one who fell while climbing the rope—were good friends. The story Joe told was that Francis was staying at his house on a sleepover one night, and Francis tried to give Joe a blow job.

It wasn't a story told, it was *crowed*. It spread like wildfire through every crevice of the bored school. Francis stayed home and laid low for a week. But when he returned, the savage disgust (his act not even provable; I have a slight doubt that he really was gay) had not abated.

In gym we were choosing wrestling partners. Francis was matched with Rick Charles. "I'm not wrestling with a faggot!" he protested to the Emperor Barrett.

"God, sorry Rick," said the Emperor Barrett, "I totally forgot. I wouldn't want to touch a disgusting creep like that either."

What happened after that? I don't remember. Did Francis flee? Transfer to another school? He's not in my yearbook. I am sure I shunned him as completely as everybody else did, which wasn't difficult. He showed me what can happen if you exhibited an enthusiasm for anything out of the ordinary. I would keep my mouth shut about the modern sculpture planted in our town square, my enjoyment of reading Browning, and the pleasure of doing geometry proofs. Do the work quietly, and correctly, and get the hell out. This was the motto of the Incredible Shrinking Man as he fought the spider with a needle for a weapon: kill or be killed.

The Emperor Barrett, to this day, is still in power. During the holidays, I was handed a clipping from the *Citizen-Patriot*, coverage of the festivities surrounding his Lifetime Achievement Award. Emperors, czars, pharaohs are all raised to believe that they are part god. Aging even when I was thirteen, the Emperor Barrett boasted that no matter how much we grew stronger in his class, he could still "take any one of you" and challenged us to a push-up contest "anytime." Twenty-five years later, he probably still blusters this challenge.

I am not so much bitter as thankful, for people like the Emperor Barrett are catalysts for people like me. I'll say it again: he sped things up. If there had been no Mr. Barrett, I might have lingered far too long in that alien landscape, trying to make myself fit in. There is a limit to the shrinking, and in the last moments of Scott Carey's story, the tiny man realizes his one great fear was wrong: "To God, there is no zero." He climbs through the mesh in the screen door and looks to the dawn of a glorious new day.

I've given up all the instruments and uniforms we use to shrink into oblivion, or avoid the snicking of the Emperor's blade. Even when I try to look like everybody else, I end up standing out like a sore thumb.

# 8

# DEATH IN THE AFTERNOON

THE TRADITION OF BULLFIGHTING—*LAS CORRIDAS*—
will not die of political correctness. It might get buried
alive, however, among the many books and articles against
the business. The outcry against the killing of bulls, a mere
six at a time, in a world where daily thousands of chickens
and hogs are bred in tiny boxes before heading for Safeway
seems a gross imbalance, and I feel cornered into a place
where I need to defend the sport.

But it's not a sport, of course—in Spain, the corridas are
reported in the Society and Culture pages, and though the
majority of my Spanish friends profess not to like the sav-
agery of the *fiesta brava*, they know the names of all the
matadors, and where they came from and how they will do
in the next *feria* (fair). This is partly due to the Spanish obsession with celebrity and the whole "cheese-stands-alone"
aspect of fame, but it also has to do with the fact that bullfighting is interesting—maybe like a train wreck, maybe like
reality television, but still, interesting. At least parts of it.

And then there are the harrumphing guidebooks. My
favorite is the *Lonely Planet Guide to Spain*, full of condem-
nation toward the cruelty and sickening nature of the battle,
which preaches for no less than four finely printed pages.

I'm reminded of an anti-gay mailing of Jerry Falwell's I intercepted years ago, in which he sent an exhaustive set of lewd pictures taken at the annual Gay Freedom Parade of boys in jockstraps, braless girls, drag queens, dykes on bikes. And if you send a donation to the Moral Majority, he promised in his fund-raising campaign letter, I'll send you even more of these horrible photos.

Well, it is odd that bullfighting doesn't step too far out of the Spanish language. The Portuguese battle bulls, but have their own rules, in which the bull isn't killed, but simply sub-jugated (humiliation, like tickling, is just a different form of cruelty) and they have a handful of bullfighters, including the recently retired Victor Mendes, who was denounced by the Spaniards (as all outsider matadors of gringo, female, or even Portuguese persuasion are) for being a *tremendista*: all style, no substance. On our side of the ocean, the Mexicans have some bullfighters, who, judging from one bad day in border-town Nogales, seem to me slipshod and horrid to watch.

But Spain: half Christian, half Moorish. Spain annually celebrates the battle between the two, and Christianity sealed its triumph by simply co-opting the *mezquites* (the elegant Muslim temples of the Moors) with cathedrals. In one of the most perfect buildings in the world, the Mezquite at Cordoba, an endless vaulted ceiling that recalls a harem tent, the Christians plopped a cumbersome church squarely in the center, making a wonderful sacred space—as even the conquering Bourbon king who ordered the structural con-version called it afterward—something ordinary.

Islam fascinates me, but, because I've been raised in a time of troubled Middle Eastern politics, it strikes me as a remote religion. Not only for its prescriptive repression of female freedom, and the warlike jihads that flare up, schismatically, there in Pakistan, now there near Israel, but for the elliptical, hermetic qualities of language and dogma that leave me outside, trying to look in. And there are all those apostrophes in words too—which I know, *I know*, are merely Anglicized approximations of another language, but still! I know they're there to denote glottal stops (an uncomfortable, masculine sound), but on the page, they look baffling: "Shi'ite," "Shari'a," "Qu'ran." It's as if everything were contracted to elide the secret, most important information, lost in the vast open space and allowed to leak out through the opening made by the wedge of the apostrophe.

I keep coming back to Spain, at least once a year. I made the Catholic pilgrimage to Santiago de Compostela and trekked across several northern provinces on foot, meeting many great friends along the way. Catholicism is just as manly, stiff, and imposing as Islam, especially in a cathedral like the one in the high-and-dry city of Burgos, a conservative stronghold where Franco felt quite at home. And why do we want things bigger than ourselves? As Browning's Andrea del Sarto mused, ". . . a man's reach should exceed his grasp, or what's a heaven for?"

In Burgos, with spires so high, the view is better than the rest of the wide-open *meseta*. As we toured the Burgos cathedral, my newfound German pilgrim friend Matthias pointed up at a gargoyle, perched high on the cathedral, as we left. He told me, "I've heard that in the Middle Ages, they sent criminals up there to put the gargoyles in place. It was a kind of punishment. If you did the task and didn't fall to your death, you were allowed to go free." For Catholics, suffering must have its redemption here on earth, as well as up above. Some people (bullfighters, pilgrims, criminals) live longer than they expect.

Backwater Burgos, like Yeats's Byzantium, is a city perfect for crusty old men. Old men, retired, have more time to attend bullfights, which are held around five in the afternoon (remember that Spain observes siesta, so that the workday doesn't really end until 7 or 8 in the evening). And while it's laughable to call one's self old before the age of forty, circumstances have made me comparably old*er*, and memoirs are mostly written about one's wild and woolly youth, when we recklessly stumbled into experiences and emotions, rather than steering, contriving, orchestrating, and buying them. The bullfights of Spain are a kind of artifice, a contrivance of experience, an afternoon's memoir, a thing for (comparably) old men who just want to generate some clear-cut emotion, see a distinction between life and death rather than experience the much less dramatic slump that bridges those two inevitabilities.

I saw my first bullfight several years ago in Seville, where I had met my very first Gypsies the year before, where bars on the windows protect the girls from their admirers and the admirers must *come ferro*, "eat iron," where the image of Faith at the top of the cathedral is a weathervane. I also saw how the grotesque reveals truths with the bullfights, and that one can have more than one emotion at a single moment— yes, sure, revulsion, but also, what is it? Now elation—now rapture—now confirmation—and now, ah, recognition.

In Seville the crowds are huge and well dressed. Men dress in full suits despite having tickets marked "SOL," in the sun. (The more expensive tickets, "SOMBRE," are in the shade.) The women wear traditional flouncy feria flamenco, or the others, bronzed and rich, wear great helmets of hair, giant gold earrings, deep bloody-red lipstick, giant pearls, and hold petite opera glasses. The men smoke cigars. I watched one of these women stroke her husband's arm through the performance; a young couple made out. The rush, or gush, of blood is a turn-on.

The ring is grand. I was ready to attend, but my guidebook with its many pages of denunciations made me feel guilty for wanting to watch. Should I stay or should I go? I almost lost by hesitating. I arrived to find all the tickets sold out, my punishment for being so ambivalent about a nation's enthusiasm. By chance I met a scalper. He had a ticket—"sol"—for four thousand pesetas. I bought it for three thousand and actually haggled, despite my language limitations.

As with opera, the cost for a seat is prohibitively expensive. You can slum at the opera by buying a standing-room ticket; there is no gallery at the corrida; the cheapest nosebleeder tickets cost about twenty bucks and go from there. As with opera, you can't be ambivalent, or you must be rich. As with opera, the bullfighting is not quite sport, not quite art, not quite natural. As with opera, it's ritual, artificial, and filled with painful, long passages of dullness while we wait for those great performances, that aria, that scene, that Wagnerian moment called *Gesamtkunstwerk*, the all-in-one melding of drama, music, emotion, and performance.

In the stands, we were piled in, without much room to move about. The sand in the ring is smoothed and ochreorange. Two concentric rings in red are the only markings. Blood, sun, sand. Three or four trumpets play an insolent, swaggering tap, repeated over the course of the three hours every time the *picadors* (the horsemen) came out. The four picadors come from behind one of six wooden protective gates. They are wearing their own fussy "suits of light," which appear to be good for maybe one bullfight of blood and sand. It seems to be the point of the fight to get close enough to the bull to get be-bloodied; the best matadors do.

Now comes the bull, a single blue ribbon pinned into his back, he's angry and bewildered. The picadors lure him to themselves with capes of fluorescent Day-Glo pink and backsides of Day-Glo yellow. I wonder if these serve to madden the bull more, these bright teenybopper colors, bubble gum and lip gloss.

As at the opera, the crowd demanded of itself total silence, until the breaks in action. If some drunk clod shouted something stupid, he was removed immediately. The mood in the arena was rather Roman, a circus: lots of thumbs up, thumbs down. When a *paso* had passed and we could all breathe for a moment, the crowd then seemed to converse with itself, deciding whether the matador had performed a good move or not; I got better at discovering what moves were good, although I was bewildered at first. It dawned on me that this is about the bull, who must die bravely. If the matador can instill a sense in the toro of having something to die bravely for, then he is a success. If a matador cannot, then it is he, not the bull, who is jeered. If he's really bad (for instance, if he can't kill the bull after three attempts), they throw seat cushions at him.

The seat cushions are renters, they can be got for a donation to the Red Cross. There's that incongruity again, when every cushion carries the trademark cross and *"Gracias por su donativo."* I thought, before this, that if one were to throw in the cushion at a bad matador, it was a kind of sacrifice. Turns out, it doesn't cost anything to throw a cushion that isn't yours.

Nevertheless, allegiances are odd at the bullfights. Even after a death-defying performance, most of the matadors didn't dare come back out to take a bow. Humility is another better part of valor. A good matador receives an ear, a great one gets a tail.

Watching the life drain from a bull is a decadent, splendorous evil. Most of the action occurs in the shade as it travels across the ring, but every once in a while, a pitch-black bull will run out in the sunlight and the blood running down his back is an effect of chiaroscuro, deep red, deep black. The colors seem all wrong—that pink cape, the red sand, and the bull's tongue is blue, you can see it even from my stratospherically high seating section. The senses have been jumbled for just a while, so that something new might be revealed to us: that's not sweat there glistening on the bull's black back, that's blood.

Revelations like that occur all the time in Spain, or not all the time, but are part of the country. You see it in the severe baroque, the leather, brass studs, whips as decoration, a sense of aesthetic beauty out of pain, the blood on the black bull. You see it in *sevillanas*—dancing that is meant to resemble the clash of matador and bull. When two teenage girls dance it, snapping their gum, it will seem like mere petulant prettiness. Two friends, a man and a woman, will dance, and it has sparks, a rush, life, concentration, heat. Then you see a couple who want each other, and there's the revelation, the sex of it, the fire and pain and severe baroque of it. Two older women will dance together, and it is graceful, warm.

So, too, the painful pleasure of bullfighting. The sun beats on your face; you've paid for this kill. "Six Toros Six" say the posters for today. Is Six Toros Six like Twenty Girls Twenty? Are the bulls all six years old? They're actually older than three, ideally, four or five years old, full of aggression and power and energy, youth incarnate. If they were people, they'd be teenagers, wanting their own phone in their room, experimenting with drugs, cherry-bombing toilets.

The bull has been snotting and frothing, now it's bleeding. Cigar smoke in your face, sun streaming. How cruel it all is. The horses are padded in a kind of mattress armor, but you can still see scars in their flanks where they've been gored. Before this century, they didn't even get the padding —they were gored, and died.

In *Death in the Afternoon*, Hemingway fills up pages and pages as he stumbles all over himself trying to explain away this ridiculous portion of the event, trying to make us believe it is not wretched, but he comes off like a husband caught with a floozy. Truly, however, this hurting-of-ponies part is the only business that I will dismiss here with disdain (but with a sentence, not a chapter). Nowadays a horse is specially groomed for this; he's had his vocal cords removed so we can't hear him scream if he's gored. If bullfighting were about reality, then why this? It's the long, unnatural road to reality—again, like opera.

Would I like such a moment, if I were a bull? The opportunity to die bravely? I think so, although I recognize it as a trashy desire, like fried chicken or gilding your house with gold leaf. I think bravery is not a necessity but something sought out. I find this belief a distressing fact in me, even beyond my attraction to the wholesale maiming and killing. Bravery is a virtue, and I guess virtue is rare. It is not necessarily innate in some beings, but it is not quite learned either. I find transvestites braver than matadors. But on the other hand, transsexuals do not even need bravery—they are compelled to simply be who they need to be, regardless of their milieu. What is the thing that is a step beyond bravery?

And are matadors supposed to instill bravery in the bull, in the crowd? Actually it's the other way around. If a matador were placed in a sealed box with a bull, some diabolical version of Schroedinger's cat(s), they would probably be sitting in opposite corners of the box, leaving each other well alone. It's the crowd—it's *me*—putting the matador between a rock and a hard place, and that's got to be some sort of consolation for old Spanish men whose joints ache after a few hours of sitting on hard concrete.

Death comes fast when the bull stumbles to its knees. A picador plunges a knife into its neck. A team of mules, gaily festooned like a Tournament of Roses float, trot out to two fat men's whips, the bull is attached, paraded about and dragged away to God knows where. Hoorah, and a kiss.

I cannot help thinking about the cruelty in terms of writers like Paul Bowles, who takes his *Sheltering Sky* travelers one by one and destroys them, six bulls six. In *Deliverance*, James Dickey's suburban weekend warriors encounter The Other, and find death. At the bullfights, I'm always sitting alone, because all my companions think I'm crazy to attend. The nature of the bullfight makes the solitude that much more intense. The true traveler ultimately wishes to travel alone. The traveler wants everything obliterated, finally, that is familiar, that is not utterly foreign. It is a kind of suicide.

But I am not a full-fledged traveler. There must remain something familiar for me. If the bull is not brave and did not rise to his destiny, a herd of tame cows is released into the ring. And as they are called in, the not-so-brave toro is absorbed into the herd, and goes out, presumably, to pasture, a mild, ignoble end, true humiliation.

And I am not naturally virtuous. I recognize virtue and it dazzles me, I love it better than evil. But it does not come naturally to me, it's something outside of me that I gravitate toward, try to recognize through description. People who are naturally virtuous—who, in other words, do not act virtuous but simply *are*—can be terrifying. There is a bull out there, I believe, that is naturally brave, who would come into the ring and not need the inciting of the matador. He would destroy the bullfights. He would be a revelation to the crowds.

But I've been watching the wrong object. It is the matador, not the bull, who should be watched. I've been watching the tenor when I should have been listening to the soprano.

I am only a part-time opera queen, so it's taken me longer than it should to discover that what opera lovers seek, besides an adored diva's performance, is not a continuous four hours of music and drama, but exquisite moments: that heart-stopping aria, that distilled emotion, that quiet gesture that weighs like star matter in the scales against ordinary life. As bullfighter aficionados seek in the corrida the perfect dance of death, opera lovers hope for one good performance.

That is why I am willing to sit through Mozart, for instance, whose work, I think, suffers from his choice of silly plots. Make no mistake: I adore *Così fan tutte, The Marriage of Figaro*, and even the occasional semi-staging of *La Finta Giardiniera*, but really, admit it: in order to match the nonsense of these farces, Mozart wrote some rather giddy patches—the mosquitoey teasing opening lines of *Così fan tutte*: "La mia Dorabella, ca-whine-whine-whine!" or the dopey recitative of *The Abduction from the Seraglio*.

And yet. Take the idiotic, misogynist *Così fan tutte*: a man bets his buddy that his own girlfriend is more true to him than the other's, and in order to prove it, they plan to leave town on the pretense of going to war—yeah, that's a good excuse, go to war!—so they can return in the disguise of, ummm, Bulgarians, in order to test the loyalties of the ladies. Madcap misadventures ensue.

But in the merriment of the farce, matched by Mozart's melodies, the drama stumbles onto its own seriousness. These men know they aren't actually going to war, but their girlfriends do not, and in the big farewell scene, there is the moment, glorious and heartbreaking, in which these ladies are convinced that they will never see their boys again. "Oh, the cruel bitterness of parting!" sings one, and the other: "My heart is breaking in two!" a lament that cannot be out-shouted by the idiotic boys singing, "I shall burst if I don't laugh!" Mozart can do nothing but drown out his own dog-gerel with the power of real feeling in that moment. And within a few bars, the stupid boys are convinced of the sad-ness too, and join in a lovely, painful quartet. It is a moment that is unearned. It comes to Mozart and then to us as a gift, and we treat it as such.

My point—the bullfight, a drama of stupid cruelty, is somehow a vehicle that now and then pulls off a profoundly unearned moment of pure emotion.

*♫.*

The second corrida I saw was in Valencia, during the crazy fiesta called *Las Fallas*, a weeklong noise-making event in which every neighborhood builds an immense statue of wood and something like papier-mâché, meant only to be burned to the ground on the last day. At three o'clock each day, I piled in with the Great Washed to see and hear the noise of the *bombas* in the Plaça Ayuntament. Every day during siesta, everybody in town gathered for the *mascletá*, a weird gender-fucked word for what it means and for how it describes itself. The word is used to refer to the insane noise of a million bombas—firecrackers by the brick, flares, and fireworks (and something they call a *borracho*, "the drunk one," a toilet-paper-tube-shaped object you light and set loose in a crowd, so that by gunpowder power it flies crazily in one unforeseeable direction, stops to fizz and smolder for a moment, then skitters off in another direction), all so loud your pantlegs flap around your ankles, car alarms go off all over town, and the physical manifestation of the noise rattles and sometimes breaks the windows in the square. And the word *mascletá* means "the feminine form of masculine," the little masculine lady.

Afterward we filed into the modernista bullring for a little death in the afternoon. Sometimes I like to make bullfighting more close to my heart by pretending it's a baseball game, a weekday game. A corrida in Catalan Valencia is different than one in Andalusian Seville. I had a Cruzcampo Brand beer cushion, for instance, instead of one from the Red Cross. The vendors in the stands sell *empanadas* and Cracker Jack along with programs. It didn't seem as hard-core in Valencia.

Whether in Valencia or Seville, I do feel like I'm always sitting in the same exact location in the bullring, which is probably due to its circular nature, and which the paranoid part of me believes means that these seats suck—though I couldn't say why. It struck me that this was a smaller ring. And there were those colors again, that red-orange, that blood-red sand. Later, on a train trip through the wild steppes of La Mancha, I'll have a thunderstruck moment when I see the sand there, naturally this color—the soil out of which grow grapes and olive trees.

People have brought sprigs of rosemary with them to the bullring, a tradition unknown to me.

The Spaniards are fashionably late. If you want them to come for dinner at 8, tell them it will be served at 6:30. But don't serve dinner to Spaniards at 6:30! Dinnertime, you bonehead, is around 11. Matinee performances at movie theaters are between 6 and 7 P.M. Enough said. Nevertheless, there is only one thing that starts on time, strictly, and that is the austere drama of the corrida. The swaggering trumpets sound.

There are three matadors today (never call them toreadors unless they're singing in an opera or you are speaking of an affected dandy), one born in 1933, one in 1962, and one in 1971—a nice generational saga, although I'm struck by how many matador retirement tours are conducted at the age of thirty-seven, which is how old I am at the moment. Yet they all look studly and alive, even grandpa Romero. The papier-mâché *falla* that is close to the bullfighting ring is huge, and you can pay two hundred pesetas to walk inside it. It depicts, among other things, a small boy being forced into the supertight pantaloons of his *traje des luces* (suit of lights), forced in to show a bigger basket. An even smaller boy is watching, and imitates him.

How normal the people in this audience look: the old guys who might haunt racetracks if they lived in the States (tatty sweaters covered by old suit jackets, threadbare trousers, well-thumbed and creased newspapers), but also Ma and Pa Kettle-de-Valencia behind me and a handful of bus drivers who just got off work and didn't have time to change out of their uniforms.

The sand has been swept into the perfect circle as if a giant protractor had done the work. On the far side of the ring, I see people wearing white cardboard on their heads like nun wimples. Some guy has put one on just like a nun, and he looks ridiculous—but this is a special apparatus for keeping the sun off. And there are always the old guys with stubby cigars.

Curro Romero enters the ring and out come the sprigs of rosemary, waved in his honor. *Romero* is the Spanish word for "rosemary." Things in Valencia seem less dusty, more vivid—Romero's cape is as yellow as a raincoat, its inner lining shocking Day-Glo pink, colors that waited to exist solely for bulls. It looks like a big sheet of candy, or disco clothing.

Romero may be a senior citizen—more senior even than these tough old birds sitting around me—but his first bull of the day is dispatched in a waltz. He bows before the bull, he kneels, he spreads that cape as if he's a butterfly, and in the end, the bull runs onto the *espada* in Curro's hand, bold enough to drive it into his own heart for an instant death. Maybe he should reconsider retirement. We are thrilled—a thousand sprigs of rosemary are thrown into the ring.

The other two matadors perform with less aplomb, and my attention drifts. A well-dressed woman—well dressed in a Madrid sort of way, all well-thought-out but just a little messed up. I mean, kelly green skirt and jacket with black stole trim and *those* bodacious pumps? She climbs across me and the precarious concrete seats with a wobbly ferocity, in the same way Spanish women don't find any indignity in riding sidesaddle on the back of a Vespa, barging ahead at a bus stop, or insisting on making a purchase when the shopkeeper is engaged in a gossip session with a neighbor.

Romero's turn comes round again. A man comes out, twirling a sign that reads "Jandilla-Leñador, 523 K." From the ranch of Jandilla, the bull Leñador—meaning "lumberjack" or "tree-wrecker" or something—weighing in at 523 kilos. The crowd cheers as Leñador trots in—you will die. But how? There are Andalusians behind me, a father and a son. It's the first youngster I've ever seen at the corridas, and I'm troubled—suddenly I'm as judgmental as a *Lonely Planet Guide to Spain*. Plus, they're noisy, talking about how Romero should take out Leñador, but I can't understand the Andaluz dialect, all those dropped endings of words, evidence to me of the enduring Muslim influence in the nether reaches of the Iberian Peninsula.

But Romero can't kill this bull. The audience, after waving their rosemary sprigs adoringly, thinks him hilarious now. I, however, am horrified as he stabs and stabs. Somebody throws in a cushion, that ultimate sign of displeasure (and it is a sacrifice, after all—these concrete slabs are hard!). Then somebody throws a Valencian orange. Whistles, catcalls. The well-dressed woman behind me can't stop laughing. Neither can the Andaluz kid. It's a nightmare of blood, a botched job. "Alé! Mataló!" the boy yells, the first thing he's said that I understand. But what he's saying is still ambiguous—"Kill him!" Is he talking to Romero or Leñador? Where, oh where, are we to look? I look up, to look away. A bird, the last one in Valencia (for what bird in its right mind would linger among the firecrackers of the mascletá and the bonfires of the fallas?), flies by, like a symbol. The boy yells "Mataló" through his rolled-up program, and indeed, Romero makes the bull drop, finally, horribly. The Andaluz father claps his son on the back.

*♗.*

Mozart was a boy genius, and never did grow old. He brought to his operas very little of life's experience, since he spent most of his in concert halls; it's easy for me to see him as one of the two buffoon boyfriends in *Così*, whose comedy comes at the cruel expense of others. But how strangely the comedy and the sadness blend in that quartet! Mozart knew only at the end of his life the many sorrows and pains that accumulate over years, that soften the rough edges. Youth is cruelly self-absorbed. Perhaps we, like Mozart, don't recognize our own cruelty until life has been a little cruel to us.

Growing older, for me, has meant learning to blend comedy, cruelty, sorrow, and a wealth of other complex emotions into a rich broth—and to recognize these odd concoctions, these unearned moments that come like grace. Let me call these moments romance. For romance, which needs a broader definition to embrace more than just the typical hearts and flowers, is what helps salvage the general misery that can be life.

Salvage. I've heard "salvage case" used to describe my friends whose immune systems have been so wrecked that they are just trying to maintain a minimal level of existence through the right combination of chemicals that aren't too toxic for the body to endure.

To say that HIV has enriched or *romanticized* my life is to oversimplify a complex puzzle of events and years that includes more than its fair share of unearned moments. These unearned moments happen more often as I get older, and I wonder why. One would think that the heart would learn to shut down in order to protect itself from a difficult world, but instead mine tends to dilate with frightening ease at the oddest things—sudden affinities, the kind I would have sneered at when I was twenty, with Kodak commercials or sappy straight-to-video movies or rococo furniture. Am I merely becoming sentimental?

By "unearned moments," I mean moments of pure and unanticipated joy. They happen most when I'm in a state of world-weariness created by the loss of dead partners, arguments with live ones, lack of sleep, or strained financial circumstances. It seems that when I am stripped of protection, it's not just trouble that I'm wide open to, but also pleasure, or a fabulous combination of the two.

The circumstances are almost inexplicable: I drive home across the Bay Bridge in the dark exhausted after a long night of teaching, and I rally as I behold the cityscape like piles of gifts. Right after an argument, my partner and I turn to each other and say the same punch line to a private joke. Rained on by El Niño once again, I find myself soaked and yet marveling at Tomatoland at the farmers' market. Pulling out my mail, I groan at the Visa bill, and then I unwrap the new *National Geographic*, which comes with 3-D glasses. Almost hit in the crosswalk by yet another annoying four-wheel drive vehicle, I look up and a pretty girl smiles at me from a beat-up convertible. The joy of these examples seems to depend upon displeasure as much as it does pleasure.

What is in life needs mediating, if we are going to have an examined life. I am constantly trying to pick things apart, dismantle them so that I might reassemble them for myself, to frame the beauty of a thing. Is that good, is that bad? I watch the improvisational ballets of macho performances like the rodeo, the boxing match, the bullfights, and I'm always finding something primal, unmediated— only the watcher can frame it, isolate the beauty, find the redemptive quality before it's gone. Could such brutal acts make artists of us all? I was so bent out of shape by the Chien Andalu, the boy who kept saying "Mataló!"—for what does he know about death? Does he know how to transform? And who am I to keep him from trying? Can there be an aesthetic education? Can Muhammad Ali or Curro Romero be called artists?

If that can be, then think of the possibilities! Lovers as artists! The man or woman who reveals the ecstasy of love to another for the first time—whatever time that would be—the dictator who storms the capital and reveals power, a scorned woman unveiling a plan of vengeance. And who will mediate these images? How can they be redeemed?

In Astorga, a small progressive town close to the rainy Galician border, I'm reminded of nearby Berkeley back home in California. There's a sanitarium in town, and the whole place is wheelchair accessible. I'm in the land of the convalescent, of the make-do-with-what-damage-you've-got. The cathedral, full of flying buttresses and more of the severe baroque I've come to love, has a little museum and sits next to a bastardized Gaudí. In the evening I sit with friends and eat under the tilo trees with our cheese and bread and good red wine. We've been hiking all day. There's time for me to sit outside and repair one of my sandals with a needle and thread. Not a very macho activity, but one that causes repeated bloodshed. I perform clumsily. Clumsiness is not feminine.

I am privy to the rehearsal of a band of trumpeters, the ones who play between the acts of the bullfights. It's a precarious sound, requiring the higher registers of the bugle. The bullfighter's horn swaggers, takes chances, sometimes fails. Notes crack. And to me, it's a beautiful, dangerous sound, a sound willing to fall on its face for an opportunity to sound glorious.

An older man in a wheelchair powered by his mouth, I think, zips by. There are plenty of things for the old and infirm to do in Spain, mostly because the old aren't shunned, not the way we shun them here (and cluck over bullfights). Every bar in the tiniest village has a gambling machine, so Las Vegas is everywhere.

Boys in these small towns, eager to escape the peace and quiet they'll gravitate to when they're truly older, practice being older. One wears a matador's Mickey Mouse hat with the artificial pigtails attached, and, to the wobbly bugle music, practices that walk all bullfighters strut, as if they were Siamese cats taught to walk on their hind legs. He is most popular among the other kids, probably because he has the hat. Unfortunately he is on the pudgy side, and I see his future, if any, in las corridas as one of the paunchy Sancho Panzas who hook the dead bull behind the mule team, festooned with pom-poms, and lead it to the butchers.

In the meantime, the old men playing *bolas*, a handful of infirm people in motorized wheelchairs, and I all watch him with envy only for his youth, an envy the boys will always be bewildered by until it is too late. We gaze at these boys the way we gaze at the matador and the bull—a little bit of life and death elegantly framed, in which it may be possible that a moment of perfection might emerge.

In my mind is good old Curro Romero, pitted against that bull that wouldn't go down. Romero is like that hoary trout living in the lake that has always escaped the anglers, with the "beard of wisdom" in the form of three or four snapped lines attached to lures hooked in his lip. He isn't a symbol of a man on the brink of death, but the endurance of life. When Leñador didn't go down for Romero, the bull, too, was a symbol of life, rather than death. The thrill of bullfights is the chance that the matador might actually die in the name of bravery, just as soldiers might die on the giddy girls of Mozart's *Così fan tutte*. There's romance there, life and love are at stake and might vanish in a quick skirmish. But an old bullfighter—well, he's lived a long life, and he hasn't died yet. It's a funny feeling, the simultaneous thrill and sadness that comes when life is served up in a generous sloppy second portion—and the stomach is already distended.

So many of us stagger around in the world, life going on when it was supposed to have left a while back—kamikaze punk rockers, now aged; HIV-positive men with maxed-out credit cards and cashed-in life insurance policies; and good old Curro. We're not very sexy, not the way an eighteen-year-old risking death is. Everything would have been so perfect if we had died young, stayed pretty.

In my youth, I was as susceptible as the next guy to the notion that life was perfectible. Just as soon as I was buff enough, smart enough, cultured enough, and as soon as I found my counterpart of equal perfection, I would have the perfect romance. But romance is far messier—and more durable—than these delicate precisions I once demanded. Romance is a mysterious scar on my boyfriend's shin, a beloved mug with a broken handle, a closed-down favorite restaurant, typographical errors in a good poem. The longer I live, the less perfect I become—and the more romantic I become.

There's a small contradiction here: in gaining experience, which is how we learn compassion and appreciate life's unearned moments, we also flaunt an innocence that we lose piece by piece. Do we suffer through disasters like bullfights, AIDS or, in a more Mozartian vein, wars, only to undo the well-woven but smothering safety net we spun through years of experience. Is the only way to innocence through experience? Aren't we better off locked in a room reading about the stuff instead? As the poet Elizabeth Bishop asks, "Should we have stayed at home and thought of here?"

No, I have answered Bishop's question for myself. No amount of book learning could make me love Mozart's operas; indeed, book learning would make it easy for me to dismiss them outright. But experience helps me to salvage unearned joy from the daily disasters. That's why I'm more than happy to watch the increasing number of gray hairs that fall in clumps each time I put on the barber's bib, and the clippers clip.

# 9

# THE MEAT MEN

I HAD BURIED THIS SECRET NEED FOR YEARS, DECADES, even. I found it was easy to hide my desires in sunny sprouts-and-pesto San Francisco—until an interloper brought me back to my dark craving. Captain Zap, scuba diver, military swashbuckler, hunky gay guy, and now my enabler, took me to The House of Prime Rib. Then I was hooked. And believe me, the first one ain't even free.

You can't pretend you are just in the neighborhood after a movie or that it was right there and you made an impulse decision. Attendance at The House of Prime Rib or any of the other red-meat restaurants in what I like to think of as San Francisco's Devil's Triangle (Ruth's Chris Steak House, Harris Steak House, along with the HOPR, are the three points that constitute my personal burning plain, and if there is any other geometric lesson to be learned from their positioning, I need only point out that the boutique store Leather 4Less is equidistant from each of the three points) requires malice aforethought—even weeks aforethought. This outing required some serious reservations. I had at least five days to think about the terrible thing I was going to do.

The House of Prime Rib never advertises, except maybe on the tops of taxicabs, the way other naughty establishments, like exotic dancers and waiters on wheels, push their dope. They don't have to advertise. They don't care about bad reviews, they don't have to care. Do crack houses care about bad reviews? Maybe red-meat establishments do advertise in secret underground Republican zines, ones we never see. In any case, steak restaurants are thriving, even in the midst of rampant vegetarianism, veganism, and people who protest the killing of slugs at the annual Guerneville Slugfest. Whatever is going on, the place is always packed, and you have to get on the list.

You get on the list, and even then, you wait in the bar area, with a requisite martini, or beer, or maybe (and this is pushing it) a blood-red wine. This wait is yet another chance to think about the naughty thing you're about to do. You sit with other Republicans, business associates, and the occasional solo male diner, all with cigars in their pockets and martinis at their elbows. You admire the redwood wainscoting, the coats of armor, the diamond-paned mock-Tudor glass, the flocked wallpaper. There are telltale decorating items—a lot of beige, certain kinds of light fixtures—that suggest the decor hasn't been renovated since the mid-seventies. Like their policy on advertising, if it's not broke, don't fix it.

🥾

Meat is all about simplicity. And simplicity is very, very macho. You kill the animal, you cut its flesh up, you throw it on the fire, and then you eat it. At The House of Prime Rib, the choices are simple: prime rib, prime rib, and prime rib. From there, you only have to decide on which cut you want. And of course, the cuts separate the men from the sissies. You can have your Henry VIII ("extra generous") to match the Tudor room, the suddenly apt beefeater statues, and the spirit of overindulgence, or select the House of Prime Rib Cut (respectable, standard), or the English Cut ("some believe there's more flavor in the thinner cut"), which is a total macho trap—you'll be revealing your innate wussiness, because less is so profoundly not more when it comes to meat. And then there is, of course, the City Cut, which is right out. I don't even think girls order the City Cut. The staff may laugh at you if you choose this item from the somewhat scary HOPR carts, shiny and domed like Dr. Who's arch-enemies, the Daleks: "Exterminate, Exterminate," indeed.

Captain Zap went straight for the Henry VIII, and I ordered the English Cut because I was the guest and didn't want to be rude. My punishment: Zap laughed at me. Heartily, Tudor style.

HOPR will serve you a fish, if you really want it, but only grudgingly. "Fresh fish of the day," it says on the menu. AQ. They started us out with predetermined side dishes: creamed spinach, spud, Yorkshire pudding (I tried to take this home in a doggie bag to be warmed up the next day, but it looked very sad and inedible by then), and a salad, quaintly served at the beginning of the meal, dressed in the house thousand-island style dribbled from on high into a spinning bowl. All of this is a way to test our mettle—were we tough enough for the great beast?

When that first piece of prime-rate prime rib hit the back of my throat (that part of the tongue scientists call the frog tongue, connected to our basest desires to kill a mammoth and roll nude on a bearskin rug and read Jean Auel novels), I involuntarily tossed back my head in some sort of glorious Cro-Magnon bloodlust awakening, not unlike what the monkey men feel in the first segment of *2001: A Space*

*Odyssey*, or Kyle McLachlan experiences when he gives Isabella Rosellini a smack in *Blue Velvet*. I was home. The rest of the evening was a blur.

Hours later, stepping out of The House into the refrigerated air that is the Bay Area climate, I was calmer, sated. Two girls wearing hemp pants walked past me and looked askance at the door swinging behind me. They frowned and sniffed, and walked on. I had been found out. I realized that if I were to have what I wanted, then I would have to keep my dark want secret, take it underground like, well, a homosexual anywhere else. I would scheme, I would get more.

A few weeks later, Captain Zap took me to Ruth's Chris Steak House. By then, I was a pro. No fussing with the steaks or marinating them or garnishing them—just red meat, with hardly a name to distinguish it. Rare. Done. Doggie bag.

That's the thing about meat: you can't give it a name. You can't call it Bossie, or Bambi's mom, or Porky, or Gentle Ben, or Granny Goose. Anthropomorphizing your food will only make you miserable. And besides, you don't call them Clancy Carrot or Artie Choke, do you? Cartoons have simultaneously stunted and ramped up our imaginations. Reality check: most likely you are wearing leather on your body, ate a cookie made with lard, or fed your dog meat-by-product today. There's glue in the book you're reading, tallow in your soap, renderings in the fertilizer in the park grass. A cow died for your sins, whether you like it or not. If indeed you are only wearing hemp pants, well, you are working very hard, and I commend you. I have no intention of working that hard, sorry.

I am ashamed, but I want more meat. So I called support: Jeremy Russell, the head of public relations at the National Meat Association, headquartered in Oakland. Did he ever get attacked by girls in hemp pants? "Actually I don't have too many good antimeat stories," Russell told me. "NMA does get protested at our annual convention in San Francisco, but the protesters are pretty unimpressive. Last year it was only a half-dozen people. One woman was dressed as the grim reaper and carried a computer printout banner reading, 'Welcome National Meat Association' in a spooky Halloween font, but that was as interesting as it got." He adds, "I do occasionally get e-mail deriding meat. They are always written with the worst grammar imaginable." Maybe the cows wrote it?

Not to be cowed by bad spellers with plastic scythes, I told Captain Zap to make reservations at the Harris Steak House, to complete our tour of the Devil's Triangle. By then my body had built up the enzymes, and I knew how to pace myself. Harris steaks come from Harris Ranch in the Central Valley of California, aged right there in the windows of the Van Ness Avenue restaurant: you can get yourself a 49er cut, rib eye, pepper steak, porterhouse, and all sorts of other voluptuous-yet-manly items: raw oysters, lamb chops, fat ol' slappin' salmon, you name it.

It snowballed—we sought out the other great meat racks of San Francisco—Brazen Head, Alfred's, and when we were broke, Sizzler. And then I bought a Weber. And in the privacy of one's own home, there is no reason to behave one's self.

🐄

I found meat nirvana at Polarica, a tony purveyor of fine game meats on Quint Street, in an anonymous dreamlike

area of San Francisco where impossible non-Euclidean
things happen—like First Street crosses Third Street.
Polarica sells elk and caribou and rabbit and boar and rattlesnake. If you want a whole suckling pig or kid goat, you
have to give them a couple weeks' notice, but they'll deliver.
They were obliging and happy to give me pointers for my big
barbecue. I purchased venison sausage, wild boar tenderloin, center cut alligator, one whole rattlesnake, tenderloin
of caribou, buffalo chorizo, and the finest ostrich steaks you
could ever encounter. It was all ranch raised, and truly free
range, according to law. They packed it up in a cardboard
box and kept it frozen with "Oncology Therapeutics
Network" ice packs, not the most appetizing choice perhaps.

The usual suspects showed up—Captain Zap, of course,
in between scuba dives, and Iowa Jill, who grew up with
Land O'Lakes Felco television ads proclaiming "Meat: Better
Than Ever!" and commemorates her allegiance by playing
bass for the fateful bluegrass band Red Meat. Her Patio
Daddy-O, Owen, who has hunted and eaten kangaroo, came.
Martha came, exacting her revenge on the bull who broke
her arm, along with her squeeze Will, plumping from all the
Irish stews Martha had been feeding him. There were also
some newbies, like Stephanie, a food critic looking for some
straight-up downscale-cuisine relief, and my landlords and
friends, Jim and Ray, who came down to "see what the stink
was." Actually, many were called, but few returned the message. "Bring chili and hot dogs, just in case we all gag," I
warned.

"Look," said Stephanie, apparently pleased, "there's
nothing green on the whole table!" No, indeed. There was
bread and cheese, and a big chocolate cake or two for
dessert, but the meal seemed more like a massive Northern

European breakfast. Friends in Munich invite me each year to a "*Hausschlachtung,*" a house slaughter, for which a whole pig is killed in early spring. Petra told me, "The boys go cut up the schwein and stuff the sausage, and the girls make sweet cakes, which is very nice because of, you know, all the blut." *You* know.

They're much more open-eyed about meat over there on the Continent, you know. Gallic expatriate Frederique explained that when we Americans look in the sky, we see Donald Duck. When a French person looks in the sky, they see Duck a l'Orange. And my Spanish friends—well! Only a couple of weeks before, I had paid a visit to the Museum of Sausages in Castellfollit, a small village in Catalonia. I had to fight through crowds of field-tripping Spanish students sampling various bits of ground-up meat.

"Oh yes," my Valencian friend Adela remembers fondly, "we used to play in the slaughterhouse when I was a little girl." Adela, for the record, is a vegetarian, but she backslid when I looted the Museum of Sausages and brought from her homeland *lomo*, a ham made from pigs that are fed only a certain kind of acorn their whole lives, under the shade of a spreading oak, massaged by a couple of farmers to make sure the marbling is perfect. Spaniards are not usually vegetarians. They can't quite wrap their minds around the concept: "So, you have the salad course, and then you have . . . another salad course?" My life in Michigan wasn't so different.

The Nuge, Ted Nugent, that rock star who lives in my hometown and holds the annual "Rape of the Hills" game-fest on his vast estate, said, "If every person went out and killed a chicken each year, the world would be a lot more peaceful place." I see his point, and as a meat eater, I feel duty bound to know just exactly what happened to my coq au vin between the coop and the kitchen, to understand where meat comes from, to not call it Chicken Little or . . . The Little Red Hen.

But on the other side of the meat argument are the equally moralistic animal rights folks, mostly urbanites who have been waiting for the spectacular plagues of mad cow and hoof-and-mouth disease, scourges of trashy country life. To the city slickers, these animal maladies are God's punishment for evil country living, the way the country folk enjoyed urban plagues, like AIDS or typhoid, which are lessons about evil urban living.

When I was a boy in Michigan, we dealt with the scandalous poisoning of cattle in the PBB disaster. Some lazy bunch of greed-heads mixed up bags of cattle feed supplement with fire retardant, and nobody knew until the majority of Michigan herds that hadn't died of the stuff had some amount of the carcinogen in their system. The chilling memory I have is of a sentence in the Jackson *Citizen-Patriot*: *if you eat meat, the chances that you have ingested PBB are roughly one in seven.* It may lurk in my body like asbestos in the lungs, or HIV in the blood. We grow our own death every day. Some of us even nurture it. Please pass the A-1.

And even without hoof-and-mouth problems, most indications are that red meat isn't very good for you, and may be carcinogenic with absolutely no PBB traces at all. For most of my adult life, I've kept the stuff to a minimum. Besides, chicken is cheaper and suits an artist's budget. But during the gold rush days of the boom economy, I lived a richer life. Hence, the spread I prepared—on that night, the Spaniards might like to know, there was no salad course at all. It's like a scene from a teutonic hunt along the Rhine. Without the guns. Or hounds. Or little cakes to cut through the, *you know*, blut.

Pretty much everything got grilled, with the exception of the gator gumbo, a fairly simple recipe I pulled off the Web. Because—and here's my whole point—if it's not broken, don't fix it. I made the mistake, the first day I got that Weber grill, of marinating beautiful tender cuts of steak in all sorts of pansy-assed sauces. That steak should have had a peppermill waved over it, and that's about it. By the time I had Owen laying down the ostrich meat, I knew there was no reason to be messing with success. I advise you to undercook the caribou, however, and slice it up into delicate medaillons. Maybe a little horseradish, but don't get fancy there, buddy.

Here's the big surprise of the evening: nobody opened the package of hot dogs. Gator tastes like a swimming chicken—maybe crabmeat. Ostrich tastes like an ultralean T-bone. Only the venison tastes gamey, but the buffalo was delicious, and so was the tender piggy wild boar. How was the rattlesnake? I just couldn't tell you. We freaked at the last minute, because it still looked like a snake, except without its skin. Adela the Valenciana has offered to make a snake paella on her next visit, but for now, it languishes next to the Chunky Monkey ice cream in my freezer.

But freezing is a last resort. As Red Meat member Jill said, "Venison is best when you eat it right after the kill, because its soul is still in it." Jill grew up on a farm and doesn't have stupid bucolic ideas of what happens to animals. Go ahead, cut 'em up and she'll be waiting at the dinner table. Except maybe for Whirlaway, her childhood pony.

According to *Dude Food* by Karen Brooks, a cookbook for ex-frat boys and sobered-up divorcés, "For most guys, subtlety is much less important than drama. It may be the turbocharge of a chocolate cake . . . or the primal gratification of sizzling meat on the backyard grill." Sometimes, like the broken clock that tells the right time twice a day, macho is right—there is no need for subtlety when it comes to cooking red meat.

There is something to be said about obviousness. Let's face it: Beethoven's music is obvious. Hubert Selby Jr.'s novels are obvious. The California figurative painters. The design of a Weber grill is obvious, too, and the design hasn't really changed over the years.

"Obvious" doesn't necessarily mean stupid, it just means that there's nothing hidden away, nothing fussy. The cards are on the table. And hey, don't forget that for all this simplicity, barbecuing meat has not phased out that element of danger. I remember using the self-lighting charcoal on our back porch many years ago, and singeing my eyebrows down to plasticky nubbins in a ball of bright flames. You lose the occasional steak to the burning coals, a sacrifice to the God of Abraham. This is the family patriarch's domain, the last Neanderthal right a guy can claim for himself. Besides, it's a lot of messy work. Owen, will you please grab the tongs? Thanks. Here's your Budweiser.

When is a macho man a sissy? When food is too weird for him. Too many spices, too many flavors, too many broths spoil the cooked. If there was something that bordered on the exotic cooked in my home, my father had to tame it with ketchup—omelettes, bean soups, even shepherd's pie.

Manly men want the basics: burgers, fries, beer. My father sometimes made dinner for us on Mother's Day or when Mom was out with the ladies. Besides being master of the grill, he was also excellent with the pancake making and the pizza-dough kneading and the spreading of frozen french fries and chicken drumsticks onto a pan and the putting them into the oven. Simple, none of your spicy nonsense, mister. Plane-food-plain. There has never been a bigger coward than a macho man presented with an eggplant remoulade poured on a bed of couscous. Or, for that matter, a plate of seafood with the head of the leviathan still attached, Euro style. Cut it off for me, Mommy, please?

Real chefs have been smart enough to see the genius of simplicity—Alice Waters, haute-chef of the renowned Chez Panisse, has more than once offered a dessert consisting of "a plate of cherries." Why would you screw around with fresh asparagus, oysters, farmer's cheese, or a loaf of warm bread? The simplicity of macho can be, now and then, elegant. Don't tell the boys.

There's all sorts of bad news here, isn't there? For macho men, for alligators, for Ted Nugent, for Bambi, and for animal rights people everywhere, who may even now be printing up their Death to Brian Bouldrey computer printout banners in a spooky Halloween font. But I believe we are part of the food chain, whether we like it or not, and to hate meat eating is to hate nature. Why these tearing teeth? Why that incredible monstrous *2001* Ape Feeling when I bite into a burger? And why, oh why, the Henry VIII Cut of prime rib?

# 10

# PILGRIM'S REGRESS

After the apostle James the Greater was martyred in Jerusalem, his followers took his decapitated body in a rudderless boat and sailed for many weeks until they landed on the northwestern coast of what is now Spain, where James, it is thought, had once preached. They placed his body on a boulder that immediately softened like wax and shaped itself into a sarcophagus. And they built a church. Beginning in the eleventh century, pilgrims have come to this shrine, Santiago de Compostela, on foot, on horseback, and, these days, on bicycles.

"BUNGEE CORDS," I INSISTED. THIS WAS NOT GOING well at all; I'd studied Spanish, but I'd forgotten about the five days I would be spending in France. Now, here I was at the foot of the Pyrenees in St. Jean Pied-de-Port, ready to begin my pilgrimage, and I needed a few last-minute supplies.

I knew the shop girl didn't know the term but I couldn't think of any other way to explain it, so I just kept saying the words over and over: "Bungee cords. Bungee. Bungee!" until it sounded foreign even to me. I'd combed the sporting goods store and it looked like they didn't have them. This was an outrage. How could an entire culture, one that boasted Proust and cheese and the Apocalypse Tapestries, get along without bungee cords?

Should I draw a picture? The girl, who was trying to be cheerful, was starting to seem afraid. She was pretty, turtle-eyed, and Basque and chose the right color for her lipstick.

I let myself have an odd thought. The people here in southern France, I remembered, embraced in the Middle Ages a heretical Catharist belief in reincarnation, a Catholic version of soul transference in which the soul, upon death, flees instantaneously and in terror to the next available orifice. How could a being hope to improve itself if passing from life to life was based on fear and not accomplishment? Oh, but that was so American of me, to think that self-improvement was worthwhile and that rigorous exercise (like a six-hundred-mile pilgrimage) was transferable to the soul.

If this girl in the sporting goods store suddenly dropped dead, would her soul flee in terror as far away from me as possible? But I needed bungee cords; otherwise, how was I going to attach things to my backpack?

"Bungee, bungee, bungee," I said again, turning to an older man, maybe the owner. He was already on the defense. "Rope? Belt? Girdle?" Just then, a tall Dutch guy walked in. "Are you in trouble, my friend?" he asked in excellent English. He was a pilgrim too; I had seen him brushing his teeth in the sink at the *refugio* and it looked like he had the bunk over me. The first thing I thought about him was, I hope he doesn't snore.

"Do you know what bungee cords are?"

He made a face. Were the Netherlands also backward?

"You know, bungee cords." I felt freed by being able to express myself in English, like a pianist who'd been forced to perform half his concert with a pennywhistle. "For jumping off bridges with. You attach them to your ankles and jump and they bounce."

The man looked horrified but instantly understood. He turned to the store manager and explained something. I was sure he used the word *pont*. Both the girl and the man joined my Dutch friend in dismay and shook their heads simultaneously, no, absolutely not.

"I'm not going to jump with them!" I spoke up. "Tell these people I'm not going to jump with them."

For a moment, the Dutch pilgrim looked stern. Reckless, clumsy Americans, smashing up their bodies with soapbox derby cars, skateboards, parachutes, fast cars, guns, and now this: bungee cords. Can't wait to get your soul scuttling off to the next available orifice, can you? "Rope, you want rope." The Dutch man made some motions, and took over. I didn't mind. He handed me the rope after the purchase. "Now you can secure your sleep sack."

"Sleeping bag?" I said. "I don't have a sleeping bag."

"Do you think you are being manly just because you want to jump off bridges and sleep without a sleep sack?" he asked. He pulled me back to the sporting goods store for a second purchase.

♣.

I walked with Loek, the Dutchman, for the first two days out of St. Jean Pied-de-Port, a traditional starting point of the old road to Santiago. He must have thought I was the dopey naive American incarnate: I'd come without the sleeping bag (several guidebooks suggested that they were a good idea, but not required), my pack was too heavy, and now this—THIS!—I'd walked into Spain without a single peseta.

I don't know what I was thinking, except that perhaps Roncesvalles was a town, not just a monastery. I had visions of the way tourist towns go: restaurants that honor Visa, Coca-Cola machines, and a convenient ATM installed in the side of a church. After all, at the monastery in Samos there's a gas station; in one of my most beloved photos a shrine of the Virgin rises above an overloaded Dumpster. Somehow, to my dismay, Roncesvalles has remained pure.

We'd crossed into Spain on a Saturday. Even if the villages we passed had banks, it was Sunday now, and everything was closed.

At lunchtime in Linzoain, a tiny village that venerated Saint Saturnine, Loek said, "Good thing I am taking care of you," and bought our *bocadillos* with the pesetas he'd had the foresight to change back in St. Jean Pied-de-Port. I let him chide me, although I would have liked to point out that he wouldn't have gotten his sandwich exactly the way he wanted it if I hadn't ordered for him. Loek knew a lot of languages, but not a word of Spanish.

From around the corner came a *romero*, a Gypsy, with a rucksack. He sat down next to us at the picnic table. I'd dealt a little with Gypsies in Seville the year before. If they managed to get their sprig of rosemary into your hands, you were doomed until you gave them money. Of course, I knew all about the practice of mistrusting Gypsies, but for El Americano, Gypsies were mostly theoretical rather than the nuisance Europeans had made them out to be. I watched Loek shut down, as I fearlessly made conversation with the stranger, practicing my Spanish and asking curious questions. He was a curiosity. First of all, he was cross-eyed.

Second, he was traveling alone, something I don't think many Gypsies do. Most importantly, he was a pilgrim, but traveling in the opposite direction, away from Santiago. The perversity thrilled me.

"I'm going to Rome," he explained. "I hope to be there by Christmas." He'd left Santiago on July 25, Saint James's Day. He showed me his pilgrim certificate, the *compostela*, something I looked forward to getting myself. He had a pilgrim's passport, he was for real, but he was going to all the places we had already been to, and he was eager to tell me about all the places I'd be going to.

He pulled out a folded, tattered list of refugios he had stayed in and began to rate them for me. He told me a tantalizing story about the hostel in Ribadixo, hundreds of miles away in Galicia. Next to it he wrote, "Dream of Peregrino." He said something about rowing out to an island in a river, where the refuge was beneath—what? I was struggling with my Spanish—a trapdoor? I imagined a wide lake, a castle in the middle, a boatman transporting Christians to safety for a coin. Arzua, *muy mal*. Puente la Reina, *muchos gentes* (Arzua is very bad. Puente la Reina has a lot of good people.) All the way down his ratty sheet, he'd write in *sí* or *no*. He handed me his list as a gift.

I kept talking to him, and Loek looked askance. He didn't like my encouraging the Gypsy, and kept studying his own little guidebook. The Gypsy, whose name was Jesús, wanted to know about the refugios in the other direction, what could he expect? Did he have to pay? Would they understand his Spanish? He asked me, "How do I say this in French?" and wrote on a slip of paper, "Could you please give a pilgrim some money?" In English, sounding as naive as I could, I asked Loek, "How do you say this in French?"

Loek narrowed his eyes and slipped on his backpack. "I am going to get a head start," he said. "Since you are so fast, you will catch up to me soon."

The barkeep came out, perhaps out of concern for me, left alone with the Gypsy. I wondered whether Jesùs could see it, was he used to it, did he always get this reaction wherever he went?

In the Middle Ages, Gypsies surged into Spain because of the Camino de Santiago. The pope had given the king of the Gypsies a letter to carry with them, giving them access to every inn and church along the way. "Please take care of these good people," it said. "They are God's children, and there will be a reward for your hospitality in heaven." The Gypsies took advantage of this letter for hundreds of years before anyone wised up. The barkeep wanted to know, Is everything all right here? Do I need to get rid of this guy for you? But what he said out loud was, "Anything else to eat?"

I wanted to show I was comfortable with the situation. I had my backpack pinned beneath my knees and if he really wanted my walking stick, I'd find a new one eventually. "Café con leche, por favor," I said. I would catch up to Loek fairly quickly.

"Un bocadillo de queso," said Jesùs, and the barkeep looked at him. But he went in and made the cheese sandwich.

I turned to Jesùs. He pointed at the slip of paper again. I said, "I think you say, 'Donnez-moi d'argent.'"

"Bueno," he said. "Donnez-moi d'argent."

"Sí."

He looked at me with those crossed eyes. "Sí. Donnez-moi d'argent." I laughed, despite the situation. "Oh, I see." The barkeep came out with his sandwich and my coffee. "But you see, I don't have any. Truly, none at all. In fact," I suddenly realized in my absentminded state, "I don't have any money to pay for this coffee." I must have looked panicky.

This is when I experienced my first true Miracle of Santiago. Jesùs, my Gypsy friend, who had already given me his secret list of refugios, pulled a small coin purse out of his pocket and motioned to the barkeep, who stood in the portal of his little shop, draped with that curtain of beads meant, I guess, to discourage flies from coming in. He pulled out the pesetas and motioned at my coffee and his sandwich. *"Todo junto,"* he stated, "all together." And he paid for my coffee.

Essentially, a Gypsy had given me money. The barkeep looked as astonished as I was.

Jesùs got up, slipping on his *mulchila*—his backpack. "Gracias," I kept saying. "Buen viaje." He said the same to me. I turned, invigorated by unlooked-for generosity and café con leche, and scampered off, eager to catch up with Loek and tell him about the miraculous occurrence.

It wasn't until I caught sight of Loek on the road ahead that I realized my pockets were full of francs, a currency now useless to me, but the very thing my Gypsy friend needed.

And the Gypsy's gift was one that kept giving: the piece of paper with his scribbles and ratings turned out to be dead-on accurate. We learned to avoid the places he had written *no* beside, and sought out the ones he'd written *sí* next to. It became known, among my fellow pilgrims, as The Gypsy's Guide to Santiago. Of all the pilgrims I met on the road to Santiago—the quack Italian bone doctor, the Madrid bull-fighters, the Frenchwoman who carried all of her things in two shopping bags, the Brazilian pilot—the one who haunted me most was the cross-eyed Gypsy, alone, walking against the flow. His goal had come and gone, and yet he struck me as the more authentic of us, the solitary sojourner who had turned desire into longing, removed the objective from his sight, and continued, anyway.

From the very beginning of my journey, the road markers had constantly reminded pilgrims of how many kilometers there were to go. For the last one hundred, there would be stone markers announcing every single kilometer, like a countdown. It reminded me, among many other unpleasant things, of a dwindling T-cell count. It also warned us that we would all soon disperse, fly to our separate corners of the earth, and resume regular lives. One of the phenomena of the last five days would be the multiplication of blisters among my fellow pilgrims' feet. I took these wounds to be a sign of reluctance, of a resistance to the coming end of our journey, a statement, by the body, of its unwillingness to reach point zero.

How free the cross-eyed Gypsy must have felt, without the burden of those numbers.

.𝓁.

Since A.D. 700, pilgrims have been coming to Santiago from all over the world, walking the same path I'm walking, complaining about their feet, telling jokes with other pilgrims, looking forward to that day when we all arrive at the Portico de la Gloria in the cathedral and get our compostela, a certificate that, more or less, gets you a third off purgatory.

But why were we still making the pilgrimage? I was afraid that I'd be surrounded by religious fanatics, but so was everybody else. With a few exceptions, we were all agnostics, or unsure Catholics, mutually agreed that we're stuck with this religion and going to Santiago to find out if there was any way to make peace with it. Loek, forced into retirement by Shell Oil, was hoping to find something else to do with his life.

For three days, we had walked along with five Belgian men, who mostly kept their distance in the evenings, but who were very talkative during the day's hike. I got to know Pietr well, one of the three who were taking orders from the other two. Every morning, the two order-giving ones, both short, blond, and taciturn, would say in Belgian (therefore I approximate), "Okay, you guys, time to get up, let's get moving." Pietr and I talked for three days about our mutual interests—opera, literature, travel, good wine.

We passed by Irache, a vintner famous for giving free wine to pilgrims. You simply filled your travel cup with as much as you could drink, just as long as you didn't steal. Unfortunately we'd arrived at nine in the morning. This didn't stop most of us. But when Pietr reached for his collapsible cup, one of the two phlegmatic blonds said, "No, stay away." Pietr frowned, and obeyed.

I furrowed my brow and asked Pietr, "Why do you take orders from those guys?" Pietr smiled. "Well, you see, I am a prisoner."

A prisoner? So were the other two men who were taking commands. No shackles, no firearms, who could tell? It seems a Belgian law that dates back to medieval days allows criminals to be punished by sending them to Santiago. My fellow Belgian pilgrims were doing penance, with the added punishment of fixing church doors along the way.

"What did you do?" I asked Pietr.

He never told me explicitly, although I heard further down the trail that all three were embezzlers. "White-collar crime," is all he would tell me. "So," I thought it out, "if you're going to Santiago as a punishment, why am I going?"

Pietr was amused. "Oh, Brian, you haven't heard?" He explained it to me: "When you reach Santiago to receive your compostela, you are also given a coupon from the archbishop. This coupon you may use to commit a murder." We all laughed. "One murder," he clarified, "or two armed robberies."

The Belgians stopped in Viana that day to fix a door. I never saw them again.

My journal contains lots of reasons I was going to Santiago. For the cultural history. For the architecture, the exercise, the friendship. One murder, two armed robberies. The main reason, the dramatic one, the true one, however, had slipped away, because I was no longer going to die, at least not tomorrow.

I'd watched my partner, Jeff, and many other friends make desperate moves to thwart death: they'd changed their blood, ingested the poisonous essence of peach pits, and submitted to the pharmaceutical shakedowns that can only be referred to as severe baroque—a word I'd use to describe the cathedral in Burgos as well—only to succumb to the virus anyway.

I hadn't been sick enough to plunge into any of these risk-taking activities, but I had had my own crazy seat-of-my-pants lifestyle: no savings, no 401(k). I'd thrown all my money into travel: I'd gone nude waterskiing in Alaska, climbed down sheer cliff faces in the Italian Alps, and stowed away on trains into Portugal. Santiago was one more—or one last—notch in my bedpost.

-&-

I'd also thought of *The Canterbury Tales*. The holy blissful martyr was said to heal the sick, if you came to see him. The cast of characters I met as I walked across Spain rivaled Chaucer's ribald gang, including Sandy, the completely deaf translator of four languages; Gabriel, the retired photographer of the great bullfighters; and Dani, the twenty-something Mallorquino who'd read more American literature than I had. Many pilgrims I met were going in hopes of miracle cures.

I had already had the miracle cure! At least I had had the miracle staver-offer—the antiviral cocktail of three blue tablets, one brick-red capsule, and one little white diamond that looks like the French Bar-Tabac signs I'd seen north of the Pyrenees.

Another miracle that my dead friends could never have imagined is how painless these pills are. Clean as a whistle, although a two-month supply to be hauled over the mountains and across Spain did, for a while, seem heavy. But, in any case, no stomach-rotting failed remedies, no diarrhea, no headaches, no nothing.

I am not usually a fan of miracles, or miracle makers. Magicians dazzle me, all kinds. A skilled writer, an excellent musician, a good lover, a chef, the ones who overpower the senses and make my imagination go limp. I don't really want my imagination to go limp. The rest of me, body, intellect, soul—these are sloppy and inconsistent, but if only I could discipline my imagination. Yet I often yield without hesitation to those who can make me slumber in the present without thought of past or future, because they don't need me to do any of their work.

Santiago's miracles are more subtle. He awakens the imagination and revives the sleeper until the past, the present, and the future are all one.

🐦

Matthias Machnik, my excellent copilgrim from Ger many, has been thinking about a good many things on his walk to Santiago. He is a hardworking Munich engineer who has been taught that "Arbeit macht frei," and a man must be responsible, stoic, and yet able to discuss with intelligence economics, world affairs, and soccer. He was raised in Düsseldorf in the shadow of the Bayer factories. A year ago, his father was diagnosed with cancer and died a week later, no doubt poisoned by the very machinery that put Brot on the Tisch.

Knocked for a loop, Matthias almost staggers down the camino. Since the coming together of the European Community, my companions all share the same economy, and when we talk about our work back home, the merrymaking Spaniards seem to be having a lot more fun than Matthias is at his ten-hour-a-day job. And is this any way to be a man?, he asks me, all this strutting around in flashy clothes, matadors stuffing their trajes des luces with socks; how can men be so vain? And now he has discovered that one of his pilgrim friends, the dopey bungee-jumping American, is a great big sissy.

But Matthias likes to enjoy himself in Spain. He likes the big dopey sissy. The two of us are walking a long stretch to the big city of Burgos, that city with the huge cathedral and bullfight aficionados.

He thinks out loud to me, "When I was a boy, my father took me out into the street and threw a ball at me as hard as he could, over and over. It would hit me, but he forbade me to cry, because I needed to become a man, a strong man." We walk a few meters in silence, and a couple of frogs jump into the swampy canal at our side. Then Matthias says, "Stupid German stuff."

At the outskirts of Burgos, beyond the POLIDEPOR-
TIVO (the sports arena), is the great bullring. And in the
parking lot of the bullring, there's a big farmers' market with
baskets of apples, peaches, and perfect, glassy, voluptuous
cherries.

We buy a bag of them. Our Swiss compatriot, Jean-
Philippe, and Matthias try to see if they can shoot the pits
out of their mouths over the walls of the bullring, which are
about two stories up. They were getting a lot of height, but
not quite making it. Petra took a shot and she wasn't bad—
"for a girl," said Matthias. Then it was my turn.

I did my windup: if I'm going to make a fool of myself, I
want to be in control of the foolishness. I made as if I were
getting a running start, as if this would help my trajectory.
The pit barely looped out of my mouth and hit my shoe.
Everybody laughed; it's always horrible, even when you
know you're going to make them laugh. But Matthias made
the "sign of the egghead," which I had shown him days
before, arching my hand over my head to show what I had
been as a child in a family of athletes: hopeless, nearsighted,
uncoordinated.

With his stocky, Hunlike body, Matthias has a low center
of gravity, good for childbearing if he were a woman, good
for combat as a man, excellent for a pilgrim; he is like a
load-bearing beast and not easy to push over. He bashes
through life, too busy to think of the consequences.

The two of us were sight-seeing in Burgos. Burgos is like
all of Spain boiled to a concentrate, full of that severe
baroque machismo. There's mostly a military history to
Burgos—it's been a bunker more than once, for El Cid, for
Franco, to name just two. And the colors I remember most
are deep red and deep black, the colors of a bullfight, or a

Nolde painting. Burgos is the cruel humor of Don Quixote. It's the sharp austere lines and Moorish patterns that forbid representational figures. All thinking is abstract, geometric: which patterns will constitute a plane? This, this, and this, and no other. The knives of the banderilleros, matador, and bull, Moor and Christian, they all participate in it.

Thus the obsession with fire, with knives, with blood. Cigars smolder, heat is barely kept under control. Burgos is all that, and the cathedral at the center of it all is the epitome of the epitome.

After so many warm, intimate churches, Burgos's seemed muscle-bound, Inquisition-style. It was a church built to show the world a manifestation of strength, and it was a success on that count. We walked through a sprawling space, squat for a church that was meant to soar. The library at my old university was similar in shape, and Frank Lloyd Wright had called that, scornfully, a pig on its back. The cathedral in Burgos had that quality.

In one room we beheld the famous crucifix of the Cristo de Burgos, said to be made of human skin but actually sewn from bull hide. It was appalling, yet riveting, like a bullfight. There was a golden representation of Christ's family tree, and the tomb of El Cid himself. Still, there were all those grinning devils and pagan effigies. It didn't seem like a holy place—not so much because of the devils, but for the way it seemed meant to spook us all into Catholic submission.

But I didn't say that out loud. I kept accentuating the positive. There were some beautiful stained-glass pieces and an airy dome, a vault of stars called the "lantern" that seemed to go straight to heaven. The whole central area was surrounded by horizontal bars, keeping us out or something very menacing in.

"It looks like a prison," I dared to mutter. I didn't want to offend Matthias, perhaps he liked the strength of the place.

"God, yes," he almost gasped with relief. I realized that he was holding it all in—he had been disliking it just as much as I had but didn't want to offend me either. Once we realized that neither of us cared for this sort of style, we pitched full force into it, or rather, we mounted a crescendo of distaste for the cathedral. It couldn't do a thing right. Look how it fails here, look how unhuman that is; see the way it was built for giants and not for us. Now we—Matthias and I—are an inseparable conspiracy.

Though I feel perfectly nonexistent elsewhere, I am on stage as a pilgrim. Perhaps this is another test of the camino, to be both ascetic and inward and also on display to everybody we pass: villagers, tourists, sinners, saints. Matthias and Petra were sitting exhausted near a fountain in Logroño one day, and a busload of German tourists surrounded them and began to shoot photos and riddle them with irritating questions. One fat man asked, "Don't you wear the cockle shell only after you have arrived in Santiago?" He had a shell around his neck because the bus, complete with air-conditioning, microwave, and toilets, had transported him conveniently to the Portico de la Gloria three days before. This was another test of the camino.

Matthias snapped back at the picture snappers as a bulb blew in his face, "We are not a deer park!"

Matthias, like me, feels more comfortable as an invisible man. He is uncomplaining about the hardship of walking forever, even though he has a hangover half the time. But he has a fussiness to him in his exacting ways. Like the Spaniards we dine with, he has a phobia about spiced food. If it is arranged on his plate in the wrong way, he is suspicious. He knows his soccer statistics to the decimal point, the way my brother knows baseball scores.

Nicole, a French Basque pilgrim from Saint Jean de Luz, has found what many of us consider the perfect male companion: a man who is sensitive enough to cry but too much of a man to really do it. This is her Spanish Basque husband, Gabriel. Nicole is an opera buff, and that is what the two of us discuss when we walk the road together. But her husband is a retired photographer who specialized in catching the great bullfighters in action. When he wants to understand my rudimentary Spanish, that is what we talk about.

Nicole is so girlie, it is to laugh. And Gabriel is so macho, he is as fussy as Matthias is finicky, Proustian in his narrow band of severe baroque ideals: hard liquor every night, Basque politics, bullfighting. He suspects my cupcake proclivities, if he doesn't already know for sure. I can see it in his eyes. I don't know how he'd treat me if I weren't as thick as thieves with the others.

In San Juan de Ortega, Gabriel nearly breaks my heart when he dances with nine-year-old Maria, dubbed the Princess of the Camino. As I'd seen in Seville among the bulls, the Sevillana casts the man as a matador and the woman as a bull meeting its fate, one of Eros and Thanatos. The way Maria played it was so intent, a kind of puppet show or foreshadowing of something that would happen later in her life: meeting a boy, courting, skirting, avoiding, submitting with grace to the inevitable.

We watched with Maria's parents, an evidently blueblood Madrid couple who were both dentists. They watched the Sevillana with both pride and—concern? Gabriel was the matador extraordinaire. He seemed to realize as much as I did that this dance was not merely cute, but had shadowy cautions. He showed restraint—any good bullfighter's duty is to allow the bull to die bravely.

Maria also had a big preteen brother, Carlos, who hates the Camino de Santiago with all his premacho heart. He is doing it on bicycle while his family is on foot, and what he ends up doing every day is riding way ahead of us and then riding back again out of frustration. Ironically he'll do the whole pilgrimage twice. He's furious because he's been lied to—this is two weeks in and mom and dad dentists have promised him only a week of this nonsense and then a trip to the resort town of San Sebastian so that he can go surfing—I asked him if he was a goofy-footer and he knew exactly what I'd said. He also knows what bungee cords are, and that's how he connects with me, a fellow Extreme Sports Guy. Otherwise he would have to face the fact that he is in the filthy, dusty *meseta* with a bunch of old people, including me, and that's not high adventure, not at all.

It was in San Juan de Ortega, it occurs to me, that I made several small discoveries, or was awakened to many things that had been going on for the weeks along the camino. The pilgrimage is like one long look into a mirror. With so much time for self-reflection, but also stripped down to nearly nothing, it is more directly easy and necessary to take an ongoing account of one's own body and its failings.

"I think I've got a hernia," I wrote more than once in my journal. For some reason I was convinced that the daily shouldering of my backpack had caused a groinal collapse (it didn't). There were the other pains, like the place on my collarbone where I'd broken it several years before. The strap of my pack put pressure on the burr where the bond had re-fused, and by midday, it would often get sore. And of course, there was the problem of the feet.

Pilgrims dropped back or dropped out by way of the feet. An ill-fitting pair of boots could ruin you. We'd lost Loek at Logroño; we'd all marveled at the way his right foot had swollen into a science-fictiony shape. Jean-Philippe longed for a new pair of shoes.

One of the more macho men from Madrid, with whom I had discussed the reason I liked Madrid more than Barcelona (big shoulders, real men), had, in Fromista, a terrible problem with his foot, involving infected blisters. The local doctor told him that it would require a bit of minor surgery.

"Let me get a drink before you operate," he told the doctor, "to handle the pain and steel my nerves."

We went along with him to the bar as a gesture of solidarity and we took turns buying him shots of Jota-Bay *escoches*, sometimes joining him. But the more drunk he got, the more frightened he was, until finally he fled the bar, fled the refugio, the doctor, and ultimately the pilgrimage.

It's unfair to compare the deadly stunt of mountain climbing to the more plodding rigors of a pilgrimage. But there are similar elements of egotism and hubris, more salient perhaps because a pilgrim is supposedly walking in the spirit of penance and humility. A mountain climber can brag about summiting Mount Rainier. The way a pilgrim tends to put it is something like, "I can't believe I just did that."

From the moment I approached my pilgrimage, I became paranoid for my body's well-being. In the waiting room of Paris's Gare du Nord, I watched for the train to Bayonne while suspiciously eyeing the reckless operator of one of the Zamboni-like floor polishers, sure it was going to careen out of control and run me down, ending my pilgrimage before it even started. Every loose cobblestone, every piece of cheese sitting out in the sun too long, every dog off its leash was a potential ruination. And yet the whole trip was some kind of endless body thrash, a way to see how much mine could take.

Everything is almost stupidly simple on the camino. There is the road, there is a pack, there is the body. Perhaps the feet are a separate item, but it gets no more complex because of them. The pleasures are simpler too, so that I found myself approximating the joy soldiers say they feel, or athletes, or matadors, a clarity that seems bloodthirsty.

I am attracted—erotically and aesthetically—to the hard-living, the slightly damaged through danger-seeking. Scars thrill me, and broken bones too. My late partner, Jeff, who died at the tender age of thirty, was not so tender. He wrestled, and had such a high threshold of pain I am guessing it was a fatal flaw.

The blemishes he got from carpentry, the nicks and cuts and swellings, were added to the ones from roughneck body slams on the mats—and later to the purple bruises of Kaposi's sarcoma, chronic folliculitis, and rampant warts. How do I say without disgusting the reader that up to the last day, I was attracted to his beat-up, beaten-down body? "Rode hard and put away wet," he'd say of himself, or more accurately, his body—a phrase relegated to ill-treated horses on the Illinois farm he grew up on.

When he died, what could I do? Imitation, they say, is the best form of flattery. In his absence, I needed a replica. Why not myself?

How unromantic an HIV diagnosis is compared to other ways of living dangerously. People climb Mount Everest when statistics say one in every three attempts ends in death. And yet they are noble madmen and women. Soldiers are brave, matadors are artists, pilgrims are holy. A man who gets HIV is stupid, weak, cowardly, poison. There are no romantic songs about HIV.

But the result is the same: when a body knows that it is riding on the brink, every adventure may be its last. I spent the years between testing positive and the successful use of new drugs living out all my fantasies.

*❦*

> In the Middle Ages, when a pilgrim came to Santiago, he made his visit to the cathedral, and then continued on to Finisterre, the end of the earth. There he would toss his old clothes into the sea and begin the long journey home.

Something else extraordinary happened in that masculine city of Burgos, where I toured the cathedral with Matthias. That afternoon, hiking in, my backpack felt light. This was supposed to have been a grueling day, but I was full of energy and I couldn't figure out why. Twenty-eight kilometers must have been a miscount! I'd been so nervous about the toughness of the day's journey—and the lack of coffee—that I'd forgotten to put on sunblock.

After a shower at the hostel, Matthias's wife, Petra, and our Swiss friend, Jean-Philippe, went into town to shop for new walking shoes. Matthias and I suggested we meet them in the Plaza Mayor after we had visited the cathedral.

It was only when we finally met up with the other two that I really started to limp.

I ordered a fizzy lemon soda. Petra gave me an aspirin.

"You look terr-EE-blay," said Matthias.

"I feel terr-EE-blay," I said. "Did you find shoes for Jean-Philippe?"

I was in pain, but I could see that the Plaza was pleasant. Everybody was out on it. Petra amazed me. She wore that damned Indian cotton-print skirt again; she always managed to make it look slightly different, hitching it up, pulling it in, accessorizing. She joked with me now and then about having her nails done or slipping out for a bubble bath or shopping for some high heels, but she loved this, the simplicity of it all. For that, I thought, she was a beautiful woman, one who can make a couple of bracelets, a little lipstick, and that same old Indian skirt look new every evening.

In the Plaza Mayor, locals talked with their friends and had a glass of wine. There's no such thing as prime-time television in Spain, and nobody seemed sorry about it. I wasn't.

But I was hunched down. I must have let loose a groan, because my friends looked at each other with great concern.

I started to shiver. I said I should go back to the hostel. Petra said she would go with me, since she wanted to get some food for the next day. Jean-Philippe said he and Matthias wanted to look in one more shoe store, but then they would bring some sandwiches back and we could have an early dinner and I could go to sleep.

By then the aspirin was upsetting my stomach. I followed Petra into the market just off the plaza. I felt achy and feverish. It must have been sun poisoning. Sunstroke or sun poisoning? I always got the two confused. In the *alimentario*, it was warm and airless. All the wheels of manchego cheese in the room were ripe. My ears began to buzz, and I got dizzy and started to sweat from head to foot. "Estoy muy enfermo," I said, calmly. I had a strange out-of-body view of the situation, which, my assessment was, could not be helped.

This must be what happens, I thought, when you faint. I'd never fainted before. "Hay servicios?" No, there were no bathrooms, but perhaps in a bar down the street.

Time was running out. I ran into the street, if only to get away from the warmth and the smell of cheese.

Once out of the store, the dizziness increased, and I noticed a little kid on a dolphin-shaped mechanical ride, the kind you put a few coins in and it bobbles up and down to carnival music. This one played a relentless passionless incessant version of "There's No Place Like Home," over and over and over. It was like one of those over-the-top scenes in a Tennessee Williams play, in which the main character's sanity, exposed as a house of cards, tumbles down before your very eyes, and the demented calliope toodles on and on and the funhouse mirrors shiver and all the world is laughing and jeering and there's no exit from the room and then—

And then I barfed into a planter. And felt instantly better.

Petra saw the whole thing. She patted my back and handed me a third lemonade. She'd gone through with all her purchases, even though I was vomiting in public. What else could she do? She had a loaf of bread and three small sweet buns, a can of olives, and a wedge of cheese. Ten minutes before, the sight of these things would have made me barf. Now that I had anyway, now that I'd gotten the poison out of me, I was starving. "Can I have one of those buns?" I begged her.

I think it relieved her that she could do something. I kept saying, "I feel so much better. I feel so much better."

We walked along the river. It was early evening. She wasn't saying anything. Looking back, I think she was terrified.

I said, "I forgot to put on sunblock today."

"Stupid boys," she said, blaming the foolish bravado of my sex rather than me, which didn't sound true to either of us. That's the thing about never fully qualifying for the badge of macho: you can't depend on he-man bonehead courage, the fools-rush-in heroics of masculinity, to cover up for your idiocy. You yourself have to take the blame for your own bad judgment.

The river babbled. Petra wanted to say something, I thought, maybe to soothe me, but she was at a loss. I was trying to think of something to say to reassure her that the illness was over, that I felt 100 percent better, which I really did. She handed me a second sweet roll. "Brian," she said, reluctantly, "we think you should stop the pilgrimage."

"Stop? Why would I do that? I just did a Stupid Boy thing, I just forgot to put on the sunblock."

"We have heard about how you are dying."

"Dying?" I sputtered, and stood stock still under a huge stone tablet declaring that it was here, here on this spot, that Franco took control of Spain, O, Peregrino.

Suddenly everything made sense. Somehow, somewhere along the way, I had told a fellow pilgrim about my HIV status. When was it? At the drunken dinner Loek and I shared in the Basque village? Under the influence of *pacharan*, that devil's drink? It was Loek, the Dutchman, I was sure. I'd probably told him when he was at his brattiest, complaining about being an old man. Maybe I wanted to eclipse his little drama with my own, to shut him up once and for all. (It never did work.) But wouldn't I have told him the whole story?

For weeks now they must have been fretting about me, always watching the poor dying boy, who was always laughing and telling funny stories but was secretly in pain and not long for this world. Smiling on the outside, crying on the inside. Oh, brother.

I set her straight. I told her everything I knew. When I first planned my pilgrimage to Santiago two years before, I thought it would be my last hurrah. My T-cell count had gone down to the level at which I had to start cutting back. I had imagined myself using the last of my strength to sojourn to . . . to do what?—to thank Saint James, to thank somebody, for the good if short life I'd had. What a nice bit of closure, I had thought, an ending that I could control, no matter what fate might ultimately deliver.

But a year before the trip, I got into a study for the then-experimental protease inhibitors, the drugs that turned out to work like a charm. By the time I set out for Spain, my T-cell count had climbed to the point it had been years before, and, while my health had never been failing, I had become a pilgrim possessed of all the strength and vitality of a man who'd escaped death, at least for a while.

Now, I told Petra, my pilgrimage was not to thank St. James for a life well lived, but for a second life, the one I hadn't thought I was going to have. "I can't quit now, Petra, because this is not the end for me. In fact everybody wants me to start my life all over again."

She had torn off a little bit of bread. She wasn't weeping, but she was full in the throat with a kind of joy that I hadn't experienced myself over this revelation, because it had not, until this moment, come upon me so dramatically, so collapsed in time. When I saw how she saw it—that I wasn't going to die, that I was going to live, I thought to myself, yes, you are right, what a happy ending it actually is. Let the new beginning begin. When Jean-Philippe and Matthias got back to the hostel, Petra must have run out to tell them. They gathered around my bunk, where I'd already taken a sleeping pill in hopes of getting a long night's sleep, being surrounded, as we were, by a fleet of German cyclists. Matthias wanted to toast my long life—ugh, with pacharan. They were so relieved, they made me feel relieved for the first time in many years.

$\clubsuit$

I met Sandy very late in the game, in O Cebreiro, a tiny Galician village at the top of a mountain with round-shaped thatched huts called "pallozas." The church there has a twelfth-century statue of the Virgin Mary that is said to have once miraculously inclined its head.

Sandy has joined us at dinner and she sits quietly. When I finally ask her something, she asks that I repeat it, and when she responds, she speaks in perfect BBC British-English. "My mother is English and my father is Spanish," she tells me.

Sandy is pretty and charming. She actually speaks four languages, and is in fact a translator by profession. And she is totally deaf. "I didn't speak until I was five," she said, "so my parents thought I was retarded." When we walk, Sandy has two walking sticks, so she looks like she's cross-country skiing.

It's the last day. We are approaching Montjuic, Mount Joy, the hill from which pilgrims get their first glimpse of the glorious cathedral of Santiago de Compostela. Petra, Matthias, and his brother Andreas, who has joined us for the last hundred miles of the walk, are at this high point, and the guys are smoking cigars in celebration. Matthias gives me a drag. I hand it back and he pushes it to me again. "Einmal ist keinmal," he says.

Sandy translates: "'One is nothing.' If your friend says 'Come with us for a beer' and you say, 'Just one,' you say, 'Einmal ist keinmal.'"

José Luis, a photographer, walks up to us—he shouts at the site of the glorious spires of the grand wedding cake, our imminent reward, rising from the rainy Galician fog. And keeps on walking.

I turn to Petra, because we're confidants by now. "Que piernas," I tell her, what legs. She agrees.

Matthias rolls his eyes. Sandy asks Petra, "What are your three important criteria for a man?"

"Tall," says Petra, looking at squat, stocky Matthias. "Musical. Blond."

"I am blond!" says Matthias.

"Einmal ist keinmal," says Petra, and we laugh. He gives her a spousey nugey. We all begin our descent into Santiago.

"So you're gay?" Sandy asks me, more direct.

She's asked and I'm so joyous, it's like alcohol, and so I think I'll tell her everything, the whole problematic story, which few other pilgrims know:

I spend about fifteen minutes giving all the grisly details. Then I start to think out loud to her. It happened because of all my weaknesses: sloppiness, inconsistency, a lack of rigor, an unwillingness to play by the rules. I gauge a person's intelligence by these things, and by my own measure, I am a moron.

We were walking single file down the trail, and the city unfolded like a rose before us. "And I came to Santiago," I told her, "because I thought it would be the last strenuous thing I'd ever be able to do." Then I rattled on about the new drugs, and how they were working for me.

I told that to Sandy. I told her all my reasons for walking to Santiago, just blurted it all out, how I thought I might die and now this had been postponed, and my new quandary, my new pilgrimage, the new language I had to learn to speak, the language of the future.

"Have you ever been in such a situation?" I asked Sandy. She was silent. Had I shocked her? Told her too much? Was she stomping ahead of me in quiet disgust? I had been walking directly behind her so that our conversation was slightly more private, but now I caught up with her, to see if I could get a hint as to what she thought of my big sob story, if I would be forgiven or offered words of wisdom.

She saw me look with appeal at her face and she said, "I'm sorry, did you say something?"

Sandy hadn't heard a word I'd said. She'd turned her hearing aid off. The bells in the cathedral began to chime. We'd arrived.

♫.

A British naval captain gives a toast: "Sweethearts and wives," he begins, raising his glass solemnly. Then he shouts, "May they never meet!" and we all laugh and chug our pacharan. We were on a post-pilgrimage pilgrimage, all of us marveling at ourselves for having actually done it, all six hundred miles of it; are we crazy or what? We were on the "Paris-Dakar" run, a long alley of bars named after cities along the course of that famous road race. The point is to have a drink in every bar along the street, the last at the finish line in Dakar.

I looked down at the ground as I trundled off to the next bar, and it didn't seem important—paved, gravel, grass, mud—who cared now? It reminded me of Elizabeth Bishop's poem about Robinson Crusoe after he was rescued, how he had prayed every day that his knife would not break while he was marooned, but now it was useless, destined, at best, only for a museum.

There had been an urgency to my life that, now that the danger has been (at least for the moment) avoided, baffles me. I don't know what to do. Growing old used to be an impossible object of desire. Now the promise of early death has evaporated. Now I am the cross-eyed Gypsy going to Rome.

Finding something on the other side of Santiago is the challenge in a life that I had decided long ago was going to be miniaturized, but has suddenly telescoped out. Should I be sad about having an empty dance card?

We were all a little sad on the Paris-Dakar, even though Jean-Philippe had bought us a bottle of pacharan and Petra had publicly incinerated her cotton-print skirt. Matthias and I took to commiserating about sex. "Look at the Brazilian." He points to a man we had dined with a week before and who had impressed me with his ability to speak several languages perfectly. He has reappeared at a table with a handful of beautiful women hanging on his every drunken word. "How does he do it?" Matthias wanted to know, searching for the right word in English, "With his four . . . four . . ."

"Languages?" I offer.

"No, Brian, women!" My pilgrim friends have accepted my homosexuality in this way: Brian prefers languages to women.

Tomorrow we will have to go our separate ways. In the Middle Ages, pilgrims spent a year walking to the shrine, and then, unlike us moderns, who jump on a plane, had to walk all the way home. I wonder what that would have been like: the real point of the pilgrimage wasn't to arrive at Santiago, but to arrive back home. And going home must have seemed a lot harder, more of a sacrifice.

I had walked six hundred miles in two months, my own sacrifice to time. Now time was not so much an enemy of mine, but a thing inside me like the virus. What I want to say is that it seemed strangely easier to live when there was no life left. Manners seemed absurd. So did conserving, waiting, restraining.

"When it is finally seen," laments Matthew Stadler, a writer I admire, "childhood has a trajectory, a countdown aimed toward zero. This is the sickness of nostalgia."

When we reach Santiago, or mandatory retirement, or the last T cell, that point zero has to be a beginning, not an end. Like the wall-eyed Gypsy, we must go back to where we came from, armed now, not with the joy of sacrifice, but only with the Dream of the Peregrino.

# 11

# SMACKED DOWN

THE BOOM ECONOMY CAME, COINCIDING WITH A pharmacopoeia of life-giving pills, and you'd think it would have made things nicer. Instead things looked the same way they did in the months after the 1989 earthquake: San Francisco was in scaffolding and chaos. Every available house was bought up at huge prices, and with all the extra money, the houses were getting gay new paint jobs, roofs, updated plumbing. Every escalator into the subterranean MUNI stations broke down, groaning under the weight of throngs. Gold-rush apartment buildings were being thrown up as quickly as possible. Millions of square feet of office space were not enough, and the mayor had approved millions more. Where would they all live? Every shop had a "help wanted" sign (no doubt there were no escalator repairmen); every person was doing the work of two; every apartment for one was housing two.

All of them were twenty-seven years old. Practically all of them, and those who weren't, like me, looked haggard, sailing to Byzantium. I was commuting on Caltrain into Silicon Valley in order to get the money I needed to pay for my expensive apartment. Across the aisle, a twenty-seven-year-old guy scribbled madly on a legal pad. The words were big enough for me to read, and so I did. As far as I could tell, it was an exercise assigned to him by a psychotherapist, or a minister, or creative writing teacher, to explain why he felt guilty.

"I make over $85,000 a year just to write a little JavaScript, and I don't feel like I truly deserve it."

You don't, you freak, I nearly muttered. Then I felt bad. It wasn't this guy's fault the city was being borified. In fact it felt more the fault of my own generation, the selfishness of the golden-agers, who devour the city with our weird nostalgia for a past that is, actually, another generation's. The newcomers were taking the city, but what city was it? I had heard how Italian matriarchs passed on their famous spaghetti sauce recipes from generation to generation, purposefully removing or mismeasuring one key ingredient, to ensure that the great recipe was watered down through the years. Was that what was going on here? It's hard to notice at first, when a bare-bones art gallery is replaced by a trendy restaurant. It looks like an improvement. We're hypnotized by the shiny packaging, not realizing that something of substance—a key ingredient—has disappeared.

In any case, I found myself wanting to escape what everybody else thought was the promised land. *"It was awful*, Reports Former Boom Economy Participant." I found myself making regular excursions out of the city, even to prosaic San Jose, to find fun and (dare I say it?) culture. And while San Francisco may get the Frenchified Cirque du Soleil pitching a tent in the city's great parking lot, San Francisco has passed up, or been passed over by, the most exciting circus going down: World Wrestling Federation's RAW is WAR.

♨.

I'm waiting for the festivities to begin with my friend Charlie, his wife, and teenaged son. They fill me in on all the grudge matches, explain the cross-pollenization from league to league, point out the wrestlers with the real acrobatic moves (The Hardy Boyz) and the ones who fight with pure cussedness (Justin Credible) or a wrench (Cactus Jack). While we wait, I'm reading the program: "Disclaimer: The World Wrestling Federation would like to remind you that its Superstars are trained professional athletes. You should never try to emulate what they do in and out of the ring."

I buy the five-buck program for the dance card, a kind of poetry in itself: "Last Thursday on Smackdown, Kane exacted revenge for heartbreak by tombstoning Tori as the show went off the air. Rumor has it that the McMahon/Helmsley coalition is going to get revenge on the big red machine tonight! What's instore [sic] for The Rock?"

Behind me, a little boy's novelty foam "Number 1" hand keeps jabbing me in the neck. His older sister apparently just got off the set from *Scream 3*, where she was a stunt throat. But she dreams of being in front of the camera, which is why she keeps yelling into the arena, and my ear. She's holding a sign that reads, "WCW Are [sic] Pantywastes [sic]." Over the generous three hours of RAW is WAR, I never once stop thinking about turning around and correcting her grammar and spelling.

Perhaps the only person in real danger of getting hurt at WWF events is a twit like myself who has a hankering to mill around the packed San Jose Sharks Arena with a fat black magic marker, ready to de/reface these hundreds of unedited handmade signs brought in by "The People." Some are crypto-naughty ("I'd Rather Be in Chyna"). Some are gender confused (a woman with a sign that says, "I've Got a ♥ On

For You Rock," while a guy has a sign offering his Poon-
tang). Others carry tender biblical blasphemies (Austin 3:16).
Some are too wordy ("It Doesn't Matter What My Sign
Says"). And some are just plain dunderheaded—"The Dudley
Boyz Put the M in Stupid"—funny if you're an Abbott and
Costello fan; if not, not.

I think I saw authority figures checking the signs at the
front gates—not for grammar or minor solecisms, but for
filth—and one guy wasn't allowed to take in his sign that
said, "I'm Here About the Blowjob." He sneaked it in anyway, when a friend handed it back to him over the police
barricade just as he slipped into the doors.

Pity the poor WWF: success has forced them into a
grudging legitimacy. The league picked up some of its dirt-
ier habits from the earthy, pure Incredibly Strange Wrestling
(once a mainstay of San Francisco's TransMission Theatre,
now a traveling road show since their rent increase affected
the use of the space) and for a while went below-the-belt-
south. But with their own version of the boom economy, our
guys have to clean up their act. While there are Incredibly
Strange wrestlers called The Abortionist and The Assassin,
the fringe figures of WWF are finding themselves censored,
sidelined. Take poor Al Snow, who carries his signature
"decapitated female" mannequin head. The people at Wal-
Mart, pillars of moral uprightness, decided that his action
figure must be cleaned off the shelves: bad influence. There
was a gay wrestler, but he got pulled from the Federation,
always the bad guy. Then there's the guy who keeps walking
around WWF *Smackdown!* and *RAW* episodes with a "WWF
Is Immoral" sign, a lone enforcer of the New Legitimacy.
Meanwhile, they're all going soft or something. Earlier in
the day I saw The Rock making Valentine's Day cookies with

Martha Stewart. What, as The Rock himself would say, a Jabroni.

So what's happening to the WWF? Frankly, as it gets more famous, it gets more colorful and juicy. There's more friction as the mix of ethnicities, creeds, and high and low incomes come together in San Jose Sharks Arena. San Francisco's got the bland too-many-grandmas sauce. But San Jose? That's-a spicy meat-a-ball.

There are some sparring matches going on down in the ring, but nothing important. Some of the b-tier wrestlers like Boss Man with his nightstick, Prince Albert with his prince albert come out and beat the tar out of some anonymous raw meat.

Their outfits are straight [sic] out of an International Male Clearance Catalog. Our heroes make their entrance by strutting down an underlit catwalk like it's a fashion show. When can a man watch fashion? When can a man watch ballet? When can a man watch, as my grandmother referred to her loyal viewing of *Days of Our Lives*, "his story"? When, oh when, can a man enjoy . . . camp? Why, at RAW is WAR, silly.

At least I think they're enjoying camp. I personally can't stop laughing, but maybe I'm the only one. It's as if the crowd's copped to camp, but it's adopted it as the earnest thing. Golly, it's like Henry James, writing a novel with one eyebrow arched, like The Rock, layering on the irony so thickly that it becomes something else, totally sublime, something not ironic. Sooner or later we have to take everything seriously. The methodology of Big Time Wrestling is scattershot and sloppy—but sloppy like a big wet kiss, generous, a big plate of spaghetti smothered with sauce—and rambling, a story within a story, told on the fly.

.ß.

The same day I saw the overpaid JavaScript guy on my commute, I had to leave work early for a wrestling match of my own—personal and dramatic, with no audience. At the Caltrain station in San Francisco, I waited with six other people for the bus. It was late, or broken down, or about to skid by us. Gleaming black funereal SUVs, so new they hadn't received permanent license plates yet, buzzed my face. Their drivers talked on cell phones about unfinished business, IPOs were only Pre-, everything started up, nothing finished. Their cars, where so much more time was spent these days, were the mode of discourse. So before they got license plates, they'd already applied little bootleg decals of cartoon Calvin, pissing on whatever it was the driver didn't like— Ford truck logos, Oakland Raiders, the Jesus fish. I also saw Jesus fishes a lot, and Darwin fishes too, as if some holy war was being fought. And there was that carnivorous Jesus fish I'd first spotted on a trip back to Michigan, eating the Darwin fish, survival of the holiest. I'd never seen so much religion in this heretofore pagan town.

The bus never came, and as I walked home through ground zero of the dot-com revolution, I marveled at the way the old empty warehouses were now in use. Oh, they still looked like warehouses all right—there was too much JavaScript to write to be messing around with redecorating. Plus there were months-long waiting lists to get even the lamest of contractors in to remodel; there were no receptionists, no filing clerks or grad students: this was war.

Captain Zap had to move to northerly Vallejo because his landlord wanted more rent for his room and Zap wasn't paying the market rate. Jill and Owen fled to Oakland, across the water; the band Red Meat lost their downtown rehearsal space.

"I just bought an Iowa State Fair program from 1956 with my father's veterinarian ad in it—on eBay," my friend Grant told me. In the boom economy, there's plenty of plenty. It's the age of *Antiques Roadshow* and online flea markets. This was a time of swapping fortunes, of finding the missing dish in that set of Fiestaware, the missing pawn to a chess set. All the lost would eventually be found in the new revolution. People talk about getting things on eBay as "winning." After an era of closing down, giving away, saying good-bye, we were all consoling ourselves with stuff. We deserved it, after all, having lived through drought, quake, fire, and plague. Now I was heading through the land of milk and honey to the doctor's office, not because something was terribly wrong with me, but because something was too right.

Ten years ago I had received word at a hospital clinic that I had the virus. I went through the usual backflips, and then, at the far end of the Kübler-Ross sequence, I accepted the diagnosis and decided to give my body over to science: if I couldn't live, I could at least make myself a human guinea pig for the good of humanity.

On the day I came home early on Caltrain, I was heading for that clinic again, where I'd been diagnosed and had spent long weekends over the lean years lab-ratting, participating in this and that drug study. Sue, the nurse-practitioner who had given me the drugs that ultimately extended my life, had called me for the first time in half a decade. She wouldn't tell me why, not over the phone, but I had missed her, and looked forward to seeing her again.

The clinic had changed. It no longer served only HIV patients, but all sorts of chronically ill people, outpatients, homeless, addicts; there were studies for sleep deprivation and smoking cessation. It didn't feel like a rest home anymore.

♪.

Terry the King Lawler, grandmaster of WWF, makes his entrance to regal coronation music. It's the "Gates of Kiev" movement from Mussorgsky's *Pictures at an Exhibition*, but I'm going to be smacked down if I explain that to my chairmates. Terry's got a crown and everything, and later he'll retch into it when we watch a montage on the overhead giant screens of Sexual Chocolate and octogenarian Mae Young checking into the honeymoon suite of a San Jose hotel and disrobing. Mae claims she's pregnant with Sexual Chocolate's love child. My friend Miriam advises me: "That's not possible, you know." You mean the pregnancy's not real? Next thing, you'll be telling me the fights are fake!

They may not recognize Mussorgsky, but everybody knows the next bit of music, "The Star Spangled Banner," one of the noisiest, most shapeless, octave-jumping, and obstreperous anthems around. It requires a heroically gifted voice, but making a fine singer sing it seems cruel: train your voice, so that we may torture you with this unsingable song. Miss Kitty sings it honky-tonk style, and on that phrase "laaaand of the freeee," the arena is full of cheers.

Let the games begin! The roster looks like a list of Batman's foes: D-Generation X and his woman in lavender, Stephanie McMann, roundly hated daughter of the WWF owner. Mulleted Road Dogg, Rubenesque Chyna, violet-eyed Viscera, and, OH! Ladies and gentlemen, here comes Miss! Ter! Ass!!!! Four women with signs that all read, "I'm Ms. Ass" begin to squabble among themselves.

It's the tag teams that bring out my fantasies: the Pimps and their ever-changing Ho Train of locally hired hos, the bleach-blonde Holly cousins, even the dumbass Dudley Boyz. But stupid is macho. This is a studied stupidness. Choreographed stupidity—graceful stupidity. A friend who performs modern ballet has told me how he and other dancers sometimes sit around and try to think of ways to perform an ugly move in ballet—a football tackle, a body slam. But the second it becomes practiced, it becomes ritualized, and subsequently, beautiful.

The moves of some of these wrestlers are beautiful. And yes, a lot of their moves are funny. This is cartoon violence. In tag-team bouts and free-for-alls, one guy gets thrown, ricochets off another, and creates a chain reaction that brings to mind the clicky-clacky balls on your high school guidance counselor's desk.

Artists strive to make order out of chaos, to give the messy world meaning. Storytellers piece together tales to keep us from despairing about our lives. Lately, the story of my life has been cluttered, complicated, inelegant, not very beautiful. Two distorted, bashed-up bodies in the WWF Smackdown! ring going mano a mano, with nothing but a folding chair to whack across the back of their opponent, are far lovelier and make a lot more sense to me now. Their battles are a comfort, soothing and familiar as a bedtime story.

$\triangle$

The first thing I saw in the clinic was Rigo's silhouette, hunched over two middle-aged ladies. He looks like a WWF contender, as kinky and overpumped and funny as one too. He'd been the receptionist here forever, always teetering on the brink of illness. Now his beefed-up arms were bulging out of his T-shirt, chest and abdominals defined beneath that tight fit, the show-off. The thing was: his face. It was drawn and caved and dried like a poorly cured hide, as the drugs slowly rearranged his body fat and sucked up all its moistures. All the body's challenges over the years were there to see, the acne and warts and wasting and reinflating. Scientists, it was reported, had just mapped out human DNA. I had a terrible thought: what if we all lived *forever*? Here I am, I sometimes think, something that was supposed to have gone extinct ten years ago, like the dodo, or the coelacanth, still here, looking out of place.

Rigo and I hadn't been hanging out a lot lately. I lived in the city, and Rigo lived in the cheaper East Bay. More than that, though, it was the Jack-Spratt-and-Wife problem, because Rigo can't eat food with his protease inhibitors, and I have to. Since eating is a social occasion and it's all we had time for anymore, we never quite managed to hook up for months at a time.

"You're looking great," I said.

"Don't lie." But he was flattered.

I said, "Do you know why Sue wants to see me?"

Rigo smiled. "You don't know? Oh, you're gonna *love* this one." As if it were another of his clean, corny jokes. I waited for half an hour while the understaffed office dealt with a waiting room full of what I recognized as former fellow lab rats. Everybody was looking *just great*.

Finally Rigo led me into Sue's office and took my weight. He bowed out when she came in, all frazzled business. "Show me what you're taking," said Sue. She'd had me strip down to my underwear, and I thought suddenly to myself, hey, does she have a right to do that? I got up to get my pillbox. My legs stuck to the roll of butcher paper that covered her examination table and made a peeling sound when I stood up.

No doubt about it: Sue had gotten cranky in the last couple of years. I'd heard her say out loud, "Let them wait," when Rigo reminded her that we were still in the waiting room. Now, in skivvies, humiliated, I reached for my pants, hanging from a peg, and pulled the pillbox from a pocket. The pillbox was a testament to the Problem With Generosity. All these years, I'd done nothing but relinquish and give and donate and shed. The response was: gifts in kind, including this—a silver pillbox with my initials engraved into the lid so that I couldn't donate it to anybody else, something I could take to my tomb, like a pharaoh. It was too small to carry my daily regimen of pharmaceuticals. I showed the contents to Sue, smashed into pieces so that they would fit.

I kept expecting that the pills would become, I don't know, more . . . developed, flashier, packaged. But since the day I sat in the clinic with a dock in my arm, waiting to see what the protease inhibitors would do, they had made just one color change, from pink to blue—a sex change, as it were, but still they seemed otherwise generic. As did this life transition that seemed to go on and on, unshaped, no permanent license plate yet.

"And how are you doing on these?" Sue asked. She used to smile.

Well, maybe Sue was sour because no one had respect for her. People used to respect her. But what was she? A nurse-practitioner, more than a nurse and less than a doctor. They'd done a television segment about her and a handful of other nurse-practitioners handling the overwhelming legions of sick guys back in 1992, and she was hailed as a hero. But she was suffering a kind of adolescence again: knowing too much but having less power. She'd been loved by her patients but now they were mostly gone, so what good was all that love? She was as little utilized as most of her lab equipment now, like that centrifuge over there that nearly killed her. During the study, when we were all euphoric from the preliminary results, she had been eager for it to separate the white cells from the red, and beat her hand on it, faster, faster! Several of the test tubes broke, and she cut her hand with shards wet with tainted blood. She'd had to take handfuls of AZT for a week after that accident. She never seroconverted, but Rigo told me the AZT gave her an ulcer that flared up now and then. Maybe it was flaring up now.

"Viral load undetectable," I said.

She paced. "There's something we want you to do for us." She asked this breathlessly, as if she were trying to avoid a bad odor. I had heard the same exhaling over the phone when she had called me about this appointment, and I couldn't tell then whether she'd been sighing, weeping, or chain smoking. What she was doing, though, was holding her breath—as in, don't hold your breath.

"Another wonder drug?" I asked.

"Not really," she said. "We'd like you to stop taking these pills."

I felt a soaring feeling in my body, the weightless zooming that accompanies both delight and terror. Were they suddenly discovering the side effects? A cancer, a mutation? Would my liver fall out, my sight fail?

I said, "Is there something wrong with them?"

"We hope not," she said, but she clearly didn't want to say any more than she had to.

I nodded. "A drug holiday. You want to see how power-ful the drugs are. You want to see if the virus will mutate around the drugs if they aren't constantly taken."

She didn't shake her head no. But if she had said it, she probably would have used the word "given" instead of "taken." Instead, she pulled out a manila folder and handed me an original signed release, the one I had filled out five years before, three apartments ago, one of any dozen forms I had signed during those lost years of the 1990s, holding drug companies and scientists and Sue herself harmless, The Declaration of Educated Guesses. At some point, I had stopped reading those things, the fine print, the clauses and warnings, mostly because it was generic, utterly abstract, as anything conciliatory tends to be. I was an old warehouse back then, ready for reuse.

"In 1995, you agreed to participate in this study and adhere to the stipulations set forth by the company," explained Sue, pointing to a tiny tiny paragraph. She'd obvi-ously rehearsed this moment. "We haven't taken any blood draws or monitored you, but the study never ended."

"You want me to honor a five-year-old photocopied waiver?"

"It's a legal and binding document." I asked her for a lit-tle time to sit and read the waiver. She agreed, but the moment I began to read, my eyes glazed over trying to take in the plenty that is legal jargon—a plenty that is secretly parsimonious, a prolix story poorly told.

⌁

"Neanderthal man listened to stories, if one may judge by the shape of his skull," explains our effete friend E. M. Forster. "The primitive audience was an audience of shock-heads gaping round the campfire, fatigued with contending against the mammoth or the woolly rhinoceros, and only kept awake by suspense. What would happen next? The novelist droned on, and as soon as the audience guessed what happened next, they either fell asleep or killed him."

World Wrestling Federation is back to basics—this is the "continuing story" that goes back to Dickens novels and cavemen. After a while, Big Show comes out and asks us if we remember how Boss Man verbally attacked the Show's ailing father. We do remember, we do! We were there, we were part of it! That's how WWF draws you in—it makes you part of the story.

Once again, proscenium arch drops, because the wrestler *is* us. Superwrestler Edge likes to appear out of the audience when he fights. The Rock is a man of The People. WWF is for everybody, or at least anybody who wants to get involved. If you want to crack the code and learn the story.

But look: this is elitism masquerading as populism. It's a club you have to join, are you tough enough? Nobody but us Americans allowed, that's for damn sure.

Here's how it works: good guys always win, unless the bad guys do something evil and underhanded. Some wrestlers are good guys and some are bad guys. They become bad guys when they consort with foreigners. There's a "W" in WWF that doesn't stand for wrestling, to make sure we have a nonstop supply of villains. The heavies these days are a gang with names like Benoit, Guerrerro, Malenko, Saturn—foreigners!

Poor Kurt Angle had the misfortune to be a real gold medalist from the Olympics, and this international partici-pation, coupled with the capture of a major European championship, makes him a bad guy. Also, he's not camp enough. Also, he talks too much. The good guys are men of few words. Kane only grunts. And now Kurt is out in the ring lecturing us on the great continental peoples: Suicide is down! Tourism is up! While here in poor San Jose, the prime rate is up while stocks are down. Booo, shouts the crowd. And the countdown begins for—yes!—Y! 2! J!—Chris Jericho himself. We roar! Our savior! Have you ever seen so many variations on the mullet? A woman holds up her sign: "My Name is Alexis and I'm a Jerichoholic!" Y2J has his own microphone. "While you've been lecturing us on how America has fallen into decline, America! Has Fallen! A! Sleep!"

We cheer, damn straight. We don't want no talk or legal mumbo jumbo, we want action, which is what Y2J gives us, as he dives on superclean Angle in the ring. It takes five refs to rush the ring like a herd of barber poles and pull them apart. The dust clears and there is Angle in a heap. And Chyna, Y2J's buxom bud, slips in from behind and stomps on Kurt one last time.

Most fights go like this: disqualified, canceled, sidelined, overshadowed. Did any fight stay within the ring itself? There is no proscenium arch to this play.

It's nonstop action, except during commercial breaks. The drama moves from ring to runway to stage to overhead screens.

.ᘊ

Back in 1995, I had volunteered for the umpteenth study for yet another magic elixir, and it was in Phase II trials— that meant dosage. Straws were randomly drawn, and the shortest got one tablet of the drug, medium got two tablets, long got three tablets. My straw was long. I was pleased—

while I had dedicated myself as a lab rat, I was, of course, also hoping for a cure.

The pills were pink and powdery, sissified, and had to be eaten with a stale bagel. I didn't really think about it. This drug didn't make me nauseated, though, so it wasn't like the pills I'd tested before. Immediately after taking the drugs, blood was drawn, and again every hour for eight hours. They'd inserted a dock in my arm, to save on the veins.

I knew the clinic too well. It had the cheeriness sad places always displayed, a constant parade of frosted sheet cake, taped-up greeting cards, shiny Mylar helium balloons.

I signed their waivers. It felt dangerous every time I did this, because there was risk. "Don't you want to read it?" Sue had asked.

"Fill me full of toxins. Take what you need."

She smiled, but not that tight-lipped vacant smile. "You watch too many soap operas." She permitted me to go out into the corporate garden flanking the clinic. I took a book, and another stale bagel.

It was Rigo the receptionist who came running out an hour later. What was going on? Did somebody pass out? Were the drugs killing the participants off?

"Our first results are coming in! From the first draw. You won't believe what's happening. Come now!"

Rigo pulled at my arm, the one with the dock in it. This caused the tape on my arm to pull and the dock to leak. A small orangish trail of blood followed the inside rill of a crease in the tape. We hustled in, past reception, into the lab.

"Look!" Rigo pointed to a chart, printed from a computer logarithm on one of those fancy new color printers, taped to the door like final exam grades. BB, it said, my initials. Only it wasn't a final exam, but the trail of a stock market crash, or an ill-managed company. It was the viral load, it was the number we wanted to make disappear, and it was plummeting. It was some kind of miracle so foreign it was nearly unrecognizable. I still thought it was bad news until Sue taped up four more charts.

"We're going to live," said Rigo. He said this quietly, and the quietness reminded me of the way the earthquake in 1989 had started as a low rumble.

Kablam! Shwoosh! Foom! You could not possibly fall asleep here. Most people's lives are so numbingly dull, they come to WWF RAW is WAR to be slapped awake by the pyrotechnics, fireworks, strobe effects. Even the four posts of the ring burst into flame when somebody big and thunderous, like Kane, shows up. I live in the quiet luxury that is San Francisco. Please, somebody light a brick of firecrackers and throw it in my face.

Most of my friends don't like WWF precisely for that reason: it's too loud. As we grow older, we yearn for a subtler music. I've been complaining about the thin sauce of San Francisco, and I don't want you to confuse it with a subtly flavored sauce. I'm all for subtlety: a thin béarnaise drizzle, a cottage in the woods, a Beethoven piano trio, Kawabata's haiku-like short stories. But sometimes I need a big flavor, too, I crave spice and bluster and tall mad skyscrapers and Mahler symphonies and Iris Murdoch's later, cumbersome novels.

There's a newish hero in WWF, one rising quickly to the top of the heap (I'd dare say he's second only to The Rock himself in popularity), Rikishi Phatu, whose hugh jass is dimpled like cottage cheese. They're always introducing new wrestlers, like the mysterious Tazz, or the Mexican wrestler Essa Rios. But Charlie's wife predicts Essa and his lady, Lita, are going to get old fast. Why? Because they're not very expressive. They're not emotionally available. Even Kane grunts a little, and had his heart broken at the altar.

The reason Rikishi's got a following is because Rikishi's a walking story—character, dialogue, conflict, style, all rolled into one. He has a signature dance, and we wait for the moment when he rubs that butt in his opponent's face. He's got to win to rub the butt! Go Rikishi! Plus, Rikishi's escorted by Too Cool, another erotic tag team composed of Scotty Too Hotty and Grandmaster Sexay [sic]. Marry me, Scotty Too Hotty. These men are sex objects. When The Rock takes his sweatbands off—the only other item of clothing he's wearing besides the Speedo—and throws them into his adoring audience, it's like he's doing a striptease. At the end of the evening, he makes a move like he's going to exit the ring without giving one of his Jabroni speeches. We have to scream for him to stay. He makes us beg for it. The heart dilates, I surrender. I beg, right along with everybody else.

🥾.

I was looking at the old contract Sue had put in front of me, this legal and binding document that required me to continue the life of a guinea pig.

"If that's the case, then . . ." I said, studying it, racking my brain. Then I saw it. I looked up. "How come the drug company hasn't honored this clause here?" And it was my turn to point to a tiny tiny paragraph.

"What clause?" asked Sue.

"The one where the company promises to supply the drug to us free of charge for the rest of our lives."

Smackdown. It had said that! I'd been paying a thirty-buck copayment each month to get this stuff through my insurance. The study had stopped supplying the protease inhibitor four years before.

Sue grabbed the sheet from my hand, peering at the small print, puzzling it out. And then she became defiant. Her face drew back. I studied it, her soft, white, down-covered Nordic skin pulled across fine bones. It made her appear strong without seeming harsh—and ageless, but it betrayed her every now and then when it bunched into a frown. "What about your promise to dedicate your body to science? What about your vow of generosity? Do you think I don't remember that? How we were all in it together, how we promised to help each other out? You promised." She hissed that.

I was timid and silent. Why would she want me to risk the health I'd gained?

She stared at me. I remembered her beating the centrifuge, hugging me with my positive purple slip, inserting the dock in my arm. Sue sighed again, and I wanted to fill her mouth with the words I deserved: "What has happened to generosity?"

I could only shake my head, and put my clothes on as quickly as I could. And I fled. Outside, it was a weekday, so a lot of people were at work, in their offices, and it didn't seem so crowded. November light slanted against tough surfaces, and glared. It looked pretty and merry, like a popular amusement park in the off-season. People stood in long snaky lines for hours for an overpriced dinner and surfed on couches for months waiting for a decent apartment in San Francisco. It was a resort, a pleasuredome, full of fine restaurants and sunny avenues. You came to a resort, and everybody smiled at you, as long as you paid. I could no longer count on anybody recognizing me on the street, already it was full of strangers, new vacationers, new funmakers.

I am different for rejecting fun. I'd just turned down a drug *holiday*. Resorts were indifferent, an effulgent surf that washed over the sand castle you built.

And look how young they were, these new funmakers— discovering pleasure and sex as if they'd invented it, but clean, so very clean cut, boys with video games and girls in skirts waiting for a boy to ask them out. But just as I was about to pass judgment on them all, I spotted him—a defiant Goth boy riding by on a girl's bicycle, tassles from the handlebars, which he gripped with fingernails painted black. He had a pink fur handbag slung off his shoulder with curly glitter letters stenciled over it: "I'm taken." He peddled with legs in black leggings that announced: I know all about Eros and Thanatos. It seems to me, growing old unexpectedly, that I know far less of death now than I did ten years ago.

There's something youthful about enjoying the world ending; that Goth kid with his black fingernails and lace felt it. A falling, a heartache or emptiness that's enough to fill a million pop songs.

There have got to be at least a dozen signs along the lines of "Riordan is Gay," "Herman is Gay," "DX is Gay," "Ruff is Gay," "Mike is Gay." The names are a mix of pro wrestlers and buddies back home, and I suppose the pro-fag in me ought to be gathering in my skirts about now, but all I can think is that I want to come back in April with a sign that says, "Brian is Gay." Maybe I'll get on TV, hi mom!

Mom watches. Moms watch. The backgrounds are macho: chain-link fences, cinder blocks, stacked pallets.

But there arc sccnes that occur in cheap hotel rooms and there are beauty-and-the-beast fantasies for the girls. There are explosions and pratfalls for the kids. Even little old ladies get big hunka black loverboy now and then. I love it for the storytelling; that's why I'm here. I'm a shock-headed Neanderthal who needs never-ending narrative, and here it is, a new kind of narrative with all-American heroes as inarticulate and swell as Huck Finn, rising from nothing like Silas Lapham, sexually awakening like Portnoy, braving ferocity like Ishmael or Henderson the Rain King. Only with spandex.

Why do so many of us edjimicated types dislike the fiercely lowbrow stance of pro wrestling? Um, besides the noisiness? Maybe because we didn't think of it first, we didn't figure out how to capture the attention of bored story lovers who can't stand one more bloated miniseries or tell-all memoir. We all need story to rescue us from the banality of pure chaos. We need order, a shape, so we can remember things.

The newest narrative: chaos that brings order, great emotion recollected in . . . smackdown. It is very hard not to remember Rikishi's big dimpled butt.

I'm most troubled by the spawn of the boom economy because I look at these pallid people and I think, Lordy, they wouldn't even make interesting fictional characters. That seems the great crime of my rich plain city: no character, no conflict, no dialogue, no style: the death of narrative in this new eternal life. Smackdown! is the conciliatory story that sometimes keeps me going.

# 12

# GOING TO EXTREMES

"The earaches Swift suffered from are partly responsible for his misanthropy. If I am interested in others' infirmities it is because I want to find immediate points in common with them. I sometimes feel I have shared all the agonies of those I admire."—E. M. Cioran

CATWOMAN'S BREASTS WERE GETTING BIGGER. THAT was the big scandal at DC Comics a couple of years ago, where the antiheroine finally got her own comic book. Not that her breasts were small in the first place: the premiere issue had a special "feely" bonus cover, so you could actually run your finger over the sensuous outline of Batman's foe in her slinky leotard. And believe me, she was no carpenter's dream. But with each issue the D-cup got just a little D-er, and the parents of Catwoman comics readers blew the whistle: our children's allowance money will not be spent on this!

Judging from the ensuing issues, DC Comics solved their problem by making Catwoman's hair bigger. To distract us. Kind of a Texas thing. But it wasn't the DC Comics boys who came up with the solution. It was teenage girls who wrote in suggesting the big hair escape.

The erotic possibilities of cartoons have always enthralled me, and apparently a lot of other boys as well. While many people confess that their sexual awakenings occurred after ogling a copy of *Playboy*, scrutinizing the pee-pee on a naked fountain statue, or catching their baby-sitter in the shower, I have fond memories of watching Underdog's beloved, Sweet Polly Purebread, abducted by the Moon Men and forced to make huge cakes for their pleasure. Exhausted, languid, Polly falls into the giant bowl of batter and swirls around, moving ever closer to the whirling paddles. What was that tingling sensation in my loins?

And then there was the true awakening, vis-à-vis Bugs Bunny. In a key episode, my cartoon hero is having his rabbit hole dug up by a bunch of construction workers. They're putting up a high-rise, and Bugs's house has got to go. This means war, declares Bugs, and he takes it out on the big muscled foreman, a hairy-chested bruiser with a permanent five o'clock shadow and slabbed pectorals. In the most important scene, the hapless builder finds himself standing at the end of an I beam dangling seventy stories up, balanced perfectly by a pile of bricks stacked at the other end of the beam. One by one, Bugs pulls away the bricks, and the construction worker must compensate for the weight displacement. For each brick, he has to remove an item of clothing: hard hat, tool belt, boots, jeans, shirt, socks—until the choice is removing those boxer shorts or taking the Wile E. Coyote plunge. Of course, entertainment allows violence but not sex, but every time that cartoon ran, I'd reach into my pants and hope that, maybe this time, that big hot lug would show me his 'nads and spare himself the broken bones.

Let me make myself clear: this was not one of those Mild Sublimated Episodes with Vague Stirrings; this was Full-On

Raging Boner. Sweet Polly Purebread was an example of
Mild Sublimated Episode with Vague Stirrings, but that was
just a tingling. But for my hunka hunka burning cartoon
construction worker, there was a knot in my underwear, and
at night, when I wasn't fantasizing about the Hardy Boys
breaking taboo, I thought of Bugs Bunny's mortal enemy. I'd
lie there and think of him shucking off the boots, the hat. If
he wasn't three-dimensional, everything else was: I could
smell sawdust, tar, wet cement. I could feel the vertigo in my
ears, the wind that rises when you're in high places and
makes your T-shirt whip against the skin. What was real
about him was his five o'clock shadow, the clearly delineated
pectoral muscles, the curls of chest hair sproinging about
like the wire coils of a dilapidated mattress that looked
almost like the cartoonist's afterthought.

Thinking about that—the cartoonist hunched over his
drawing table, carefully drawing every cel complete with
chest hairs; the scrutinizing, meticulous work it takes to
make a cartoon man strip to his skivvies—was a turn-on in
itself. That there was an artist out there, lost in time and
space, who paid as much attention to the hair on this man's
chest as I did, or more, was a sort of introduction to my first
ménage à trois (no matter that one of us was possibly dead,
another unreal).

But the thing that sent me over the edge was more
immediate, brutal, and selfish. A cartoon man was a comfort
to me. Like every adolescent, I had misgivings about my
body's idiosyncrasies. I wanted to blend in. I prayed to God,
that bitch, to make me look normal.

Lord knows the cartoon construction worker wasn't normal, but maybe that's why I liked him so much. His freakish
hugeness in the area of calf muscles, the permanence of his

beard, his ability to survive a seventy-story fall—compared to that, I was comfortably normal.

Exaggeration and distortion always stretch out the range of what's considered normal. Catwoman's breasts, for example. Also, Catwoman's fellow gymnast Wonder Woman has had a substantial makeover for her fresh-faced World War II body: I'd say that girl has had a major wax job. Jessica Rabbit ("I'm not bad, I'm just drawn that way") posed for *Playboy*, and later lonely laser-disc nerds discovered that she wasn't wearing any underwear if you pause the movie just right.

Parents don't understand that cartoons help us discover how to get in touch with ourselves. Nor do they understand that they reflect in some bizarre way the fashions of our time. We exaggerate to prove a point. We want to be believed. The advent of Catwoman's comic book series coincided with the bigger-is-better fashion trend, the transition from waif Kate Moss to the whole-lotta Wonderbra ampleness of Anna Nicole Smith. In the same distorted way, my construction worker was all I wanted in a man: big, big, too big. Hair, muscles, the perfect mix of strength and vulnerability. I suppose straight guys felt exactly the same way about Catwoman.

They are cartoonish, exaggerated, disproportionate, and dreamy. And ever since, I have loved the disproportionate portions of men. You think I'm joking, but my desire is real. Why bother to fake desire?

.&.

Sometimes lies tell the truth. What I mean is, when we tell a lie, we certainly hope we'll be believed. Exaggerations and lies work much the same way in fashion. Distorted images of women and their attributes, as enhanced by fashion, reveal more about our tastes than the more subtle ideals found on the average pages of *Glamour* and *Vogue*.

I'm talking about the radical exaggeration, the kind you can see in cartoons, pornography, and drag queens. Ordinary, everyday exaggerations—fashion taken to a carefully calculated, mannerist extreme—are all around. For instance, when Nancy Reagan was mommying Ronald, you could walk into any downtown office and see women wearing shoulder pads high enough to be a linebacker's, but the pads are always undercut by something—a frilly blouse, maybe, a big bow, anything that said, "I can kick Raisa Gorbachev's ass, and still come off girly." That's kind of extreme. But not quite extreme enough. Nor is the gay-boy look that has saturated teen culture, with the baroque sideburns and goatee, shorts supposedly worn through in strategic places and absentmindedly hacked off with kitchen scissors but which are in fact the result of a lot of planning and self-conscious calculation. If Lands' End can hawk "pre-thrashed" jeans, they're no longer radical, nor are they even in style.

Peoria may think Calvin Klein's fragrance for both men and women is pretty wigged-out. But wait until the big fragrance companies offer their high-end fragrances for toddlers—that'll make CK One look positively fundamentalist.

Then what is radical? I'm talking about real weirdness, stuff that makes you wrinkle your nose and say, "No way, that would never happen." Fashion science fiction. Noticing this is often a sign of growing old. When Levi's offered "hard jeans" and advertised their attractiveness by shooting a cannonball at a pair of 501's, denting the cannonball and leaving the jeans unscathed, I thought—I am old, I am old, I prefer my trousers able to be rolled.

Helmut Newton created a confession in words and photographs of his lust for the politically incorrect stiletto heel. A platinum blonde shows off some of the most monumental spikes possible, but is so hobbled by her footwear she must be photographed in a wheelchair; then, with braces; then, being carried by a hunky guy. In another, Newton painted his ladies with freakish white makeup to celebrate the fetish of necrophilia.

This is the kind of distortion that reveals. Of course it isn't real: Newton wouldn't require his girlfriend to sport crutches or paint her face White-Out white in order to appear at the dinner table, or bed, or coffin. But the truth lies in there somewhere, and he's shown his genuine enthusiasm for high heels and fair complexions by going out on a limb.

In the same way, other over-the-top images of women show us what real men most deeply desire. Take the Gaultier bullet bra, made famous by Madonna, which presents a woman's breasts as deadly weapons, or at least as something self-protective, porcupine-y, road-hazardy. Bras, like most fashion accessories today, are not for personal use but for the pleasure of others. A man's interest in the development of the bullet bra, then, reveals something about a man's vulnerability toward that part of the female anatomy. Men may seem like wolves when it comes to breasts, but they see themselves under the power of women—they can slay us, or hold us at bay, or make us infantile.

.&.

My late friend Will shared my love for the disproportionate. We were size queens together, but not of the usual sort. What thrilled us were big noses, jug ears—like a Mercedes with its doors wide open, says my Valencian friend Adela, sighing. Even the occasional protruding beer gut on the right guy pleased us enormously. When I told Will I'd had a date with Mark, a mutual friend of ours, Will was all adither. "Oh Brian," he said, tremblingly, in his Louisiana drawl, "his *teeeeeth*!"

True, Mark is perfectly built in every way: fine face, fine body, curly brown hair that looks best unkempt, redder on the chest and eyebrows, not so much legs as haunches . . . but his best feature was his worst feature. When he smiled, he became an instant poster child warning America off British-style socialized dentistry. His teeth are a mess, a ruined picket fence, crooked like old tombstones, fluoride-grayed, patched, cheaply capped, chipped. They are hot. I wanted to run my tongue across them, slice it against a misaligned incisor.

Will was always in competition with me. He wanted guys with missing fingers. Clubfeet. A guy with no legs. My own lust for the aberration is less Barnum-and-Bailey, though sure, I've had thoughts about the leather midget who suits up in his harness and roams my neighborhood. I've considered the sinewy strawberry-bepatched burn victim who swims in my lane at the Y. But I prefer the more subtle exaggerations, ultimately, the men with hairlips, tragic teen acne scars, premature gray, bowleggedness, cleft chins so deep you can store food in them. To all the boys with piercings, tattoos, meticulously shaved heads, I ask: Aren't you jealous?

◆

Alberto Moravia once pointed out that fashion is the ultimate terrorist—whole governments fall because of unfashionable ideas; men have been assassinated for outdated notions. Fashions, like terrorists's ideals, exist in time.

Science fiction's casting into the future, ironically, is usually about here and now. People in fashion have no real concern for the future and certainly must disregard the past. Take the Wonderbra phenomenon—made successful by women and the manly men who love them.

The Wonderbra's makers created publicity stunts in most major American cities that whipped up such a frenzy of enthusiasm, everybody gleefully forgot the Wonderbra was simply an underwire-support push-up bra. After women raced to the empty bins where Wonderbra once was, they moped over to the checkout counter to become number 476 on the waiting list, moping right past the huge bin full of generic underwire-support push-up bras, unfortunately not named Wonderbra, but selling for a fraction of the price.

Of course, even I, with not much interest in a woman's winnebagos, know that if you wear an underwire bra, you'll get struck by lightning.

If terrorists have a reckless disregard for the past, what do they hold in high regard? Extremism. Thankfully extremism in fashion doesn't have a body count—however many times we call each other "fashion victims"—but the radicals are the ones we should look to when trying to figure out where the future lies (or even the present).

Fashion, like terrorism, consumes as much as it can, including politics. I used to worry about the fierce depoliticization effect fashion had on symbols of social magnitude, because it rendered them merely stylish and utterly removed their resonant significance. Do these kids know, I wondered, what guerrilla fatigues were originally made for? I bemoaned dreadlocks on white guys, motorcycles called Ninjas. (Doesn't everybody want to ride a cycle whose name means "silent death"?)

But then, no matter how much political extremism the fashion shark devours, it never quite digests it all. Take, for instance, Mattel's mistake of putting a cock ring around the "Earring Magic Ken" doll's neck. No matter how much I fret that nobody knows the history or context of an object like a cock ring, I've learned to cool my righteous jets. Because sooner or later, somebody, probably on MTV, will break the depoliticized silence and tell the world, "Hey, that Ken doll has a cock ring around his neck!"

We make fashion out of politics, out of current events related to tragedy, for the same reason we make jokes about politics and tragedies. We depoliticize in order to make the most awful things bearable. In the wake of tragedy—when we manufacture Space Shuttle Challenger jokes ("you feed the dog, I'll feed the fish"), OJ jokes ("Here's your fucking glasses!"), and George W. Bush jokes (basically blonde joke retreads)—comes the flood of T-shirts defending OJ, imitating Monica Lewinsky's fashion sense with the brief comeback of the beret. I remember a decade ago when *The Simpsons* was hot and so was *Twin Peaks*, Mikhail Gorbachev came to San Francisco. Street vendors were hawking a T-shirt that depicted Bart Simpson on a skateboard, his head replaced by Gorbachev's, with the word balloon announcing, "I killed Laura Palmer." Do we need anything else in a time capsule from early 1991? But that's just mannerist, the tail end of fashion.

So what's the difference between extreme fashion and mannerist fashion? A sense of irony, perhaps, or of camp. International Male has built an empire with its catalogs full of scantily clad hot dudes wearing nothing but their underwear and Eurotrash transplant items. The clothes, for the most part, are ridiculous—and if you're ever foolish enough to order anything, you'll discover like I did, that the only way you can get away with wearing a mesh Greek-style fisherman's tank top is by being a hot enough dude to be in the pages of International Male.

But IM knows what it's doing, just like Helmut Newton knew what he was doing when he photographed high-heeled women in wheelchairs. International Male's catalog has a section celebrating its two decades in business. In illustrated sidebars, "Oh No, We Didn't!" excerpts early catalogs showing corny guys (who sure looked like hot dudes back then!) in spandex on roller skates, swinging hunks at the hot tub, bell-bottoms wide enough to store nuts in for the winter. IM laughs at itself, but we know full well that the clothes it's selling today will look just as ridiculous in the fortieth anniversary catalog. The only difference between us perceiving the silliness of the clothes and them seeing the silliness of their clothes is about twenty years. Fashion means never having to say you're sorry—at least not until about 2020.

It's not exactly breaking news to note that the fashion industry is full of subtle misogyny. It distresses me to see pictures of women looking away, askance, haughty—a tired old image of the fabled unapproachable woman. But one cannot so easily accuse an image of Catwoman of being misogynist, or take seriously the fashion directive of a big-haired, big-boobed porn starlet or dragon-lady drag queen.

Drag queens are the outer manifestations of gay men's fondest desires to be teenage girls. Many gay men had to hide their alternative desires during the teen years; once liberated, they often get stuck in a time warp where they live out that unfulfilled fantasy—in or out of a dress—of chewing gum, gossiping, and laughing at other gay men's fashion foibles, forever and ever. I was walking through my gay neighborhood one day with a friend and his sixteen-year-old sister, who was visiting for spring break. We encountered a typically outrageous drag queen dressed in a cobalt blue sequined bathing suit, complete with flippers and harpoon, and I turned to my friend's sister to gauge her level of shock. "So," I said, "what do you think of our subculture?"

She was unfazed. Between gum snaps, she reflected, "Well, it's kind of like me and my friends, only, when you guys watch *Buffy the Vampire Slayer*, you, like, *care.*"

A drag queen, like a teenage girl, enjoys knowing that it doesn't matter as much what she thinks of you—there's not going to be a wedding, so let's just have some fun. She isn't afraid to say you have a bit of a mustache problem, or that you're not looking as fine as you think you are. You can always depend on a drag queen to tell you the truth, however distorted that truth is. Drag queens aren't as misogynist as they'd like to be, because they only imitate, reflect, rather than direct. You're better off looking for fashion's progressions by studying the real McCoy: a genuine, unironic teenage girl.

No, Catwoman comics and drag queens are much closer to the realm of art than science. They are images from the funhouse mirror. Mirrors distort, art distorts. In an ill-lit room, in the heat of sex, even the self in a mirror can look strange and new, transformed. That image evokes desire, the way all the other extreme depictions of couture grab us on an animal, passionate level. You can see it in Picasso's paintings of his mistress, the loss of volume and proportion, an enormous face or breast, the distortion, the cartoonish view you get of your lover's body when you crave it and are lost in it.

When we look at porn starlets Crystal Gold or Lotta Topp we don't say, my god, I've got to catch up with them! Nor do we get imitative ideas from Picasso's jumbled mistress images. Picasso, philanderer, was called a misogynist, and maybe he was, but in those paintings, I think he was trying to celebrate the female body, not destroy it. His distorted paintings are descriptive, not prescriptive. His desire is not an artifice, it's genuine. Why would anybody fake desire?

ℛ

My late partner, Jeff, the first night we spent together, sealed our bond by slipping in a videotape of back-to-back Warner Bros. cartoons, and he did a heartbreakingly accurate imitation of Yosemite Sam. In the years that followed, he obliged my cartoon construction worker fantasies by wearing his tool belt to bed (he was a carpenter, and there is no coincidence—finally, I'd found the Bugs Bunny construction worker, made flesh).

Handsome Jeff. Unruly brown hair I'd scrutinize for hours at a time, the way it grew out straight, then curled at the ends—how was that possible? Close-set eyes of some kind of devoted animal: in the morning he'd splay like a dog on the bed. Strength in the back and shoulders, a wrestler's sense of torque and balance, Teutonic hands and wrists, thick hairy arms and a broad long chest. Jeff took his first big full-blown AIDS diagnosis dive with meningitis, a consequence of climbing through dusty ducts in that union-man drag. Meningitis, said the doctor, is not a good thing to start with. I hate it when doctors are right.

Meningitis opened Jeff up to a bad case of Kaposi's sarcoma, which transformed him as dramatically, in its way, as

any myth out of Ovid's *Metamorphoses*. And aren't all trans-
formations erotic?

Well, not at first. At first it was strange and awful: the
newness of it, the fact that he was dying and that I could
catch it, like the flu. But I couldn't help looking at those big
purple sores. They were the third party again, the scientific
catastrophe that created a new persona. Jeff was the Toxic
Avenger with a heart of gold. It was best on sunny weekend
afternoons when the sun would come through the windows
onto the bed where he'd nap like a mongrel. I'd wake him
with an exam, running my hand along a flank and circling a
lesion with a finger, zeroing in. I knew they were tender, and
he'd wake up. He'd yawn.

His mouth was so wide: he had a double-jointed jaw.
He'd grab an unattached rearview mirror from the night-
stand, something he pulled off a heap at the big
Pick-Your-Part automotive graveyard. He could fit the whole
mirror into his mouth, and together we'd look for the spread
or absence of lesions across the roof of his mouth. I liked to
watch with him. I'd hold the flashlight so we could see better and he could show me the places where it was more
tender than in other places.

Often, Will might like to have known, Jeff had his own
kind of imperfection—feverish, so hot inside. You could feel
the heat coming off him like he was a planet with atmos-
phere. And we'd both get hotter during sex, flushed, and I
noticed that those lesions—sunspots on his legs, his chest,
the bottom of his jaw—would get even more angry and bilious. Jeff would become one with the thing taking him over
and in the middle of it all, I think, at least for a few minutes,
he would take over the thing itself.

Suffering succotash, his body was beautiful, even in that

freakish disguise. I've never known a mouth, hands, torso, any and all, so well as his. Under that sheeny purple-patched coat of sores I found his skin always mysteriously smooth and lank, warm, open. To fuck with Jeff was—is—present tense. It is like driving fast on a wet curved road with trees in the path. Now his legs are over my shoulders, and I'm examining the aureoles of yellow around those glowing places. There doesn't seem to be much difference between any of our thresholds—even ears and nostrils, a little bilious.

He's stronger than me—he can flip me over with one of his wrestling moves and hold back my arms with big hands. His skin is always important. It's a different kind of skin when I touch it. Since love is an enduring close study, I scrutinize the different kinds of skin he has: the brown of nipples; the roughed-up hands. And there is that smell, the metallic smell of coins and blood, maybe a lot of vitamins sweating out from our pores. He drags his hand along my back.

Jeff is gone now (a-the-a-the-a-the-a That's All, Folks!), but when I watch cartoons I think of him. When I see a man with a missing digit, I think of Jeff. It's gotten to the point where I see anything less than perfect—the mugs with chipped handles, typographical errors, a squadron of Down's syndrome children out on the town—and I dream of Jeff.

My pleasure was for all of him. Him alone, yes, even if the virus left its own trail. The trail I chose to take: the skin, the sin of it, infected cuts, swollen eyes, the wart that never quite got burned out, the light in his eye, and the yellow corona around each lesion as they spread, eventually turning into dark sores, the way tomatoes ripen.

I don't want to say that it was right, or that it was pretty. It's not like what Mussolini's son said when flying over Ethiopia and bombing it, how he said the bursting bombs looked: *come fiori*, like beautiful flowers. I was not twenty thousand feet above; I was closer. Sometimes I was in him, sometimes he in me. I don't say it was right, or pretty, to want all of him, but make no mistake: it was all true desire.

# 13

# ODDFELLOWS

L ISTEN CAREFULLY, MY CHILDREN: THERE ONCE WAS A land not so very far from here, not so very long ago, and yet very, very different. The people there were called grown-ups, and they had telephones fastened to a building, which could only be used to call another telephone fastened to a building, usually an empty one. They did not drink chocolatey mochas or milkshakey frappuccinos, but bitter, black coffee. They did not read *Harry Potter* or *Everything I Needed to Know I Learned in Kindergarten*, but books about adult problems, like what should we do with this unwanted pregnancy or what shall we do with these unwanted children?

They were a very serious people, especially the men of this country, because as part of their inescapable roles as providers, every day they would work at jobs that often involved using machines to perform repetitive tasks, or, if they were lucky, pushing paper around a desk while wearing starchy suits with choky ties and shoes that pinched their feet. When they came home from work they were allowed to take these uncomfortable uniforms off, but then they had to do things like mow the lawn or go to a PTA meeting.

With such a dull grown-up life, the men had to create secret societies so that they could play, and so that their wives and children could not find them and make them do horrible tasks, like taking out the garbage or unclogging the toilet. To make sure they couldn't be found, at least for an hour or two, they drove to remote locations accessible by whispering secret passwords gained only after surviving mysterious initiations and receiving secret names. They met together in temples and lodges and called themselves Lions, Elks, Antelopes, and Mooses; Knights Templar of Pythias and Columbus and St. Crispin and Labor; Grangers and Gleaners, Woodsmen and Redmen, Oddfellows, Shriners and Masons. They had strange and wonderful titles like Grand Master Architect (Flava Flav's peep?) and Grand Elect Perfect and Sublime Mason (good in bed?) and the Bill-and-Ted-esque Super Excellent Master.

How much of these men's secret activities involved elaborate rituals and chanting, as is described by Pierre in *War and Peace* and mocked by Homer Simpson and Fred Flintstone, and how many of the clandestine maneuvers were really just major-kegger-dude action? We shall never know.

They kept you out or lured you in with the unknown. They started you early. I should know, because I lived among them. We boys could be Scouts or Guides or Explorers or He-Man Women Haters. I myself was an Eagle Scout and a Vigil Honor member of the Order of the Arrow and received a secret Indian name, which translates as "Active One." We wore lots of fabulous outfits. We got to wear loincloths and headdresses and sashes like Miss America. We put on plays and swore brotherly oaths and built big fires and had secret handshakes and admonitions. I was also a Rotary Club Student of the Month and wrote a speech about citizenship, which I thought was very radical, but garnered polite applause. The promise was there: if you play by our rules, as a grown man, you will always have a neato place where men can act like boys, forever and ever.

Peter Pan was a boy who never grew up. Boys who grew up to be Elks read about how Peter lived in Never-Neverland with The Lost Boys, who fought pirates and Indians and played with mermaids. "I heard father and mother talking about what I was to be when I became a man," says Peter to Wendy, the Darling daughter he steals away to be mother to The Lost Boys. "I don't want ever to be a man. I want always to be a little boy and to have fun."

Peter was sort of the Super Excellent Master of The Lost Boys, and God forbid you should cross him. He'd toss you out the second you started growing pubic hair. How great to fly and sing and lead a gang of perpetual children on raids against Captain Hook and have a scantily clad fairy bitch-slap female rivals for your sake! Think of how enviable Peter Pan must have been to J. M. Barrie, the man who invented him. Barrie was an Edwardian (the Age of Dour Dads, if anything in Disney is true), and had to spend his days frowning and withholding and judging in an even starchier suit.

Barrie's era, the turn of the twentieth century, was also the heyday of masonic organizations. "Every fifth or possibly eighth man you meet is identified with some fraternal organization," wrote W. S. Harwood in 1897. And by 1910, historian David Beito says that "a conservative estimate would be that one third of all adult males over age nineteen were members."

But over the years, things began to go wrong. Minorities wanted in. Girls, like Peter Pan's proxy-mom, Wendy, wanted in. "All I remember about my mother," says Nibs, one of Peter's Lost Boys, "is that she often said to father, 'Oh, how I wish I had a check-book of my own.' I don't know what a check-book is, but I should just love to give my mother one." Mothers wanted checkbooks, and they wanted a place in the workforce too. They stopped having their own bridge clubs and garden societies and got jobs, and then the doubly-incomed people had more money to spend on very special private suburban houses that were so well hidden in gated communities that required pass codes and were accessible only via secret codes programmed into garage doors, it wasn't long before the men felt free to make of themselves Most Excellent Poobah in their own private lodges, to buy gadgets and toys and make the house the ideal frat house they always hoped their frat house might be in college days, or the cool fort they always hoped their cool fort might be in childhood. Who needed Masons and Oddfellows when you could have a cool fort of your very own?

That, at least, is part of the theory Robert Putnam proposes in *Bowling Alone: The Collapse and Revival of American Community*, in which he describes our growing obsession with privacy and deepening sense of mistrust and loneliness, since we have abandoned all our old social groups—like Masons and Shriners.

Plenty of these groups are in deep trouble these days, says Putnam, with no "social capital" and no young folk around to replenish them. I say, Good riddance to bad rubbish. If these groups died out, so what? Who wants to spend time with a bunch of bigoted guys hell-bent on exclusivizing themselves right out of membership rosters? Most of them wouldn't have me as a member anyway.

.♣.

Recently I was asked to make a journey to a small but significant city in America's breadbasket—to be the guest of honor for their Gay Freedom activities. Middle American cities are a stronghold of all things American and grown-up, for better and for worse. You cannot cross a street without encountering yet another chapter of the Independent Order of Oddfellows or a Christian church or a bowling alley. On Gay Pride Day, about a hundred of us marched with banners down a deserted main street to the rotunda. The only people who came to watch were a handful of followers of the Reverend Fred "God Hates Fags" Phelps, a silly little man who, like a Lost Boy, thinks way too much about sex and naughtiness, and should be spanked.

For my weekend among those amber waves of grain blowing blond and golden and sepia and blond once again, my host was a kind man I'll call Joe. He's gay as a goose (are geese gay?) and also comes from a distinguished line of gentlemen farmers who were prominent for generations in the Masons and Shriners. He loved to be in the Shriner Circus, and he loved to wear the special fez and drive his little clown car that was shaped like a miniature combine. He had a little dog, too, TC, who also liked to get dressed up. Well, maybe not.

Joe loved being a Mason so much that he made it his career. The statewide office of the Masons was downtown, and for eighteen years, Joe served as director of fund-raising for the group. Every year he rounded up money for all sorts of philanthropic causes as well as cash to run the offices. Anybody who has ever created direct-mail campaigns can just imagine the address list he must have built over those years.

Then, a year before my visit, Joe's boyfriend died. Heartbroken in a King Lear Howl-Howl-Howl sort of way,

Joe basically "came out" in his conservative town by writing all about his loss in his annual Christmas letter he tucked into cards with pictures of the three wise men, or whatever. As many of you know, the letter said (and here I loosely paraphrase), mid-greeting, I lost George this year to AIDS. Hope you get everything you want this Yuletide Season. Kiss Kiss! He sent the letter to all his friends and family on his Super Excellent mailing list. All.

About a month later, an "investigation" was made on Joe. He was fired. Why? No, not because he was gay, silly, that might get your pants sued off. It was because he wrote his annual Christmas letter on the work computer. Strictly against business practice policy. They found this out because his charming and loyal secretary hacked into his hard drive and provided the evidence they needed to get rid of the homo in their midst. Of course, the canning was done in the nicest possible way. He was given a handsome severance package in hopes he'd go out without a fuss.

What could he do? It wasn't as if they were going to make working for the Masons a fun experience if he fought to stay. His life career evaporated in the course of a week. And how would they ever be able to raise money for good causes if Joe took his mailing list with him? Where would they get their social capital?

Social capital isn't always good. Beware what urban sociologist Xavier de Souza Briggs calls the "kumbaya" interpretation of social capital. Robert Putnam summed it up nicely: "When Floridians objected to plans by the Ku Klux Klan to 'adopt a highway,' Jeff Coleman, grand wizard of the Royal Knights of the KKK protested, 'Really, we're just like the Lions or the Elks. We want to be involved in the community.'" Super Excellent Grand Wizard!

When Peter is flying the little Darlings to Neverland, brother Michael repeatedly loses his power to fly over the wide ocean and hurtles toward the briny blue. Each time Peter rescues him—but only at the very last minute: "Peter would dive . . . and catch Michael just before he struck sea . . . but you felt it was his cleverness that interested him and not the saving of a human life."

Some philanthropy, we're better off without.

*♘.*

For all of its cowardice, not all boy clubs are as direct as the Masons were to Joe. Some time ago I was slated to ghostwrite the biography of my friend Poster Boy Scout James Dale, who had spent his entire youth participating in and most of his adult life in litigation with the Boy Scouts of America. Since we were fellow Eagles and Vigil Honor members of the Order of the Arrow, we made the secret signs and handshakes, and he told me all about the day the Boy Scouts booted him.

"I was heading toward my second year at Rutgers and, while I had maintained a position as Assistant Scoutmaster of my New Jersey troop, I had also come out like gangbusters." Dale was, like any best-little-boy-in-the-world, altruistic and community oriented. That's why he joined the Lesbian-Gay Alliance on campus and went to various organizations with safe-sex seminars. He was featured one day on the front page of the Rutgers school paper locking lips with another boy.

"Weeks went by, and I forgot about it," Dale told me. "Then I came home to see my parents, and my mother told me there was a piece of registered mail waiting for me." Registered mail, as we all know, is not the kind of mail we like to get.

"It was basically a form letter, sent by the New Jersey council, informing me of my dismissal. They didn't even have the guts to call me or talk to me beforehand. They promised me a hearing if I wanted to dispute, but they were so afraid to speak to me face to face, they never actually sat down with me in the same room." They, of course, were the friends and fellow Scout leaders he'd spent his entire life working with.

The Boy Scouts of America have persisted in their battle with James. While he won two trials in New Jersey's Superior and Supreme state courts, the U.S. Supreme Court (more cranky odd fellows) ruled that the State cannot require the BSA to appoint a gay scoutmaster, since it's a private group. *You* know, one of those *private* groups getting bucketsful of money from the United Way and other broad-based charitable organizations.

James Dale was dismissed on the grounds that he didn't live up to the oath he swore to the group: to be physically strong, mentally awake, and morally straight. Yet on every count, Dale has embraced the tenets of scouting far more tenaciously than anybody in his council—trustworthiness, loyalty, bravery, the whole shebang. Boy Scouts builds leadership (and by the way, they're another social organization with a crisis in leadership and volunteering) and prepares boys to be men. James Dale, for the entire eight years of his grown-up life, has been a leader, a citizen, and a man.

While most men need some private place to act like boys, James Dale has been in the public eye all this time, doing his best, doing his duty. His lawyers told him that even going to a gay disco would look bad in the courtroom. James Dale became a grown-up. Whoa, dude, how totally ironic that the BSA taught Dale how to be a grown-up citizen. They just hate it when we won't keep acting like boys along with them.

The more I see, the more I find that men acting like boys is the same thing as men acting their worst.

♌

There are some good groups around though. Groups for adults. Some of them changed with the times, or reformed. Take San Francisco's City Club, that egalitarian downtown business fraternity in one of the purtiest art-deco buildings in town. It always cracks me up to marvel at the two-story lefty Diego Rivera mural inside, homage to the plenty of California's crops and the workers who reap them, a mural that for more than half a century could only be viewed by capitalist white guys who wouldn't have known a day's hard work if it hit them on the head.

But the City Club makes old boys seem like Long Lost Boys, ancient history. They let women and minorities and gays in. Sometimes these same people are the leaders.

And you think that social organizations don't exist anymore, but there are places, and I have been to them, where people still live like that. Even right in San Francisco, playpen to the world. Chastened and revitalized by the *Bowling Alone* book, I went down to the Blue Muse and joined the Castro Lions.

After all, I come from a long line of altruistic sucker joiners. My own father is a Moose and a Lion and the Deputy Grand Knight of Columbus, which, as far as I know, means he gets to wear chain mail *and* a Stetson. My mother was pleased to inform me not long ago that he will get to be Grand Knight next, but does that mean he has to give up his badge?

In any case, the Castro Lions are just a bit different from the Lions Club my father goes to, where they have annual outhouse races and apple pie sales. The Castro Lions are the world's first lesbian and gay chapter of the club. Founded in 1985, they celebrated the fifteenth anniversary of their charter in summer 2000. They also sponsored queer chapters in Toronto and Denver, and they are beloved in the Northern California District because their delegates always come to the big annual meetings in feather boas. Take that, you silly Masons!

The Lions, in case you don't know, have made it their business to help people with eye issues. They have programs like SightFirst, the world's largest blindness prevention program. They do a lot of service-related activities not involving outhouses, and they are not against a glass of beer or a weekend in the country. The Lions have also gone coed, and one of the biggest appeals of joining the Castro Lions is having not only a big age range, but also a fully integrated bunch of ladies and gents who know how to *work* a purple and yellow vest.

Before I even walked into the Blue Muse, which is the temporary-permanent meeting place of the Lions' bimonthly general meetings (board meetings are held down the street at Marlena's, the drag queen bar), I saw the smoking members of the organization puffing away in those dashing silky vests, hanging out on the sidewalk. Some members have a bit of a biker look in those vests, especially the ones who prefer the leather version, with all their pins from various state and national conventions. Wow, roving gangs of service-oriented volunteers, loitering in the streets of San Francisco.

These folks were incredibly friendly. I walked by, I said I was looking to join, they said come on in, let us buy you a beer. Within twenty minutes I'd met half the membership (about thirty in attendance at the meeting, of a group of fifty or so active folks), and a cool officer named Michelle offered to sponsor me if I was serious.

New friends! Grown-up friends. I can't wait till I have a vest of my own, and make my hebdomadal disappearance from my regular circle of friends. I'll collect old glasses frames and stick pins in my vests. I'll have a garage sale and I'll learn the secret handshake. I'll meet cute service-oriented Super Excellent guys. How come you never answer your phone on Wednesday nights, my friends will ask me. And I'll tell them, shh, it's a secret.

Everybody needs a secret life. It's been a major goal of all of American culture, it seems, to create a secret life, or at least a private one, to build a gated community and a cool fort or join an exclusive group that's perhaps not so exclusive. The Castro Lions are the perfect antidote to San Francisco's permanent state of transition—something solid and adult in the Playpen by the Bay. As I've grown older, I've come to prefer the company of adults.

I sound like a brittle bastard for making fun of people getting in touch with their inner child, I suppose. But everything is play these days—we call sex playing, as in Playboys and Playgirls. It has an innocent ring to it. I worked for a high-tech company for a little while whose official motto was "We work hard and play hard." Don't get me wrong, fun is fun to have. But playing hard sounds a little desperate to me, something to be had at the expense of everything.

J. M. Barrie, Peter Pan's creator, was fascinated with the notion of a boy who never grew up. Of course, the magic of the eternal child is only evident when he is surrounded by other children who do mature. Wendy, in the final chapter, is a mother with a daughter not unlike her former self, named Margaret, and Peter is very pleased to abduct her, right in front of weeping mother Wendy, to that same Neverland. But as Barrie spun out his story, he realized that he had created a little monster, one more interested in his own cleverness than any concern for human life.

That is why the closing words of his book, one written for and about children, go something clangorously like this: "When Margaret grows up she will have a daughter, who is to be Peter's mother in turn; and thus it will go on, so long as children are gay and innocent and *heartless.*"

# 14

# CLEAR MOONSHINE ON AN EVENING OF WHITE LIGHTNING

O KAY, HERE'S A JOKE: A MAN PLACES A PHONE CALL. "Hello, is this the FBI?"

"Yes. What do you want?"

"I'm calling to report my neighbor Billy Bob Smith! He's hiding moonshine inside his firewood."

"Thank you very much for the call, sir." The next day, the FBI agents descend on Billy Bob's house. They search the shed where the firewood is kept. Using axes, they bust open every piece of wood, but find no moonshine. They swear at Billy Bob and leave.

The phone rings at Billy Bob's house. "Hey, Billy Bob! Did the FBI come?"

"Yeah!"

"Did they chop your firewood?"

"Yep."

"Merry Christmas, buddy."

There is nothing more patriotically delightful, whether you are a loosey-lefty or a tighty-righty, than to pull one over on the too-big, too-authoritarian government. Actually the only thing more delightful is to be a lone man single-handedly

pulling one over on the government. Ever since Boston Harbor was made into the world's largest teacup, vigilantism has been the American Way, the solitary citizen standing alone, doing it himself, a one-man army, a survivalist; he's not going to ask for directions, and he doesn't want to pay his taxes, no matter how lost or rich he is.

I don't have a compound in Idaho nor do I hoard gasoline for the coming apocalypse, but then I wouldn't exactly call myself a team player. I learned to be repelled by team spirit in the hands of Mr. Barrett the gym coach, who taught me that I, an individual, was the worst member of the team and could make the whole team lose. Teams, therefore, were a myth.

Hardly anybody is a team player anymore—basketball is getting boring and not just because they never call "traveling," but because nobody assists in a layup. Face it: Olympic runners, swimmers, whatever—these are our modern athletic heroes, and they are sexier.

So it should come as no surprise that moonshining, making your own sour mash, the ultimate federally forbidden do-it-yourself, is as sexy and All-American as hell. I drank my first Arkansas moonshine at a dinner party, and couldn't believe how, um, sophisticated it tasted, holding its own with a good bottle of Santa Cruz's Bonny Doon Cigar Volant and further mediated by these adorable grappa glasses with little glass fruits embedded in them I picked up in Amsterdam. Our buddy Mark from Little Rock, also known as Markansaw, brought the home brew from his distinguished mad scientist DIY Cousin George, who lives harmoniously with nature up in the Ozarks, brewing his home brew and keeping bees and making kites and no doubt fixing his Lawn Rebel riding mower himself and composting, as self-sufficient as an able-bodied man ought to be.

But moonshine's dirtiest secret among all the other dirty secrets is that moonshining is very *not* do-it-yourself. It's a team sport, a game of trust. The fermentation process is so expensive, time consuming, and high maintenance, there has to be an organized division of labor—one guy brings the still, another gets the grain to make the mash, somebody else supplies the secluded chunk of land, somebody watches the cooker, somebody makes the Excel spreadsheet with everybody's name and the schedule the mash is on . . . and who will help me eat the cake, said the little red hen?

The DIY aspect of moonshining has been around forever, but the problem came when a law was put up against it—prohibition. There is nothing that makes a person want to make alcoholic beverages, drink them, and get falling-down drunk than the establishment of laws forbidding a person to make alcoholic beverages, drink them, and get falling-down drunk. Alky-hawl and gubahmin have always been at odds, ever since the shameful Whiskey Rebellion in 1794, in which democracy was nearly abolished in exchange for a police state with George Washington as king. There are even rumors that moonshine made us lose the Battle of Bunker Hill—rum was running, if shot was not.

And—and this is where moonshiners could use the coming together of a couple more minds—the conventional wisdom is that if a body can make a little money off the affair, so much the better. But this is how anonymity kills: with every roaring '20s speakeasy begging for booze, unrestricted, undocumented bootleg greed ended lives. Sixty people were killed in 1928 when they were served wood alcohol; later that year, fifteen thousand people were partially paralyzed by "jake," a kind of moonshine made with Jamaican ginger. In other words, it's when the intimacy and the team spirit goes away—when moonshine gets corporate—that the stuff becomes evil.

That's why, when you talk to aficionados, you're not likely to ever get a proper set of instructions on how to make the stuff. They get all homespun and confederate on you. They compare their work to making a quilt, and measure volume in terms of "biggol" (biggol bucket, biggol siphon), distance in terms of "yonder," and weight in increments of "as much as you kin tote." If you can somehow incorporate your pickup truck's radiator in the process, this will also earn you extra macho points.

You may think they're protecting you from knowing how to make bootleg whiskey, thus incriminating yourself (the phrase "Evil to those who think it" is a mushy law covering all sorts of suburban knowledge, from the production of opium out of garden poppies, to the distillation of ethanol from garden juniper berries, to the expanding of your property line simply by mowing your neighbor's grass). But legally you can make up to a hundred gallons of wine or beer in your home, per person, and still be a fine upstanding citizen. Distillation, however, the rendering of hard liquor, now that will win you a trip to the clink. It's the distillation *recipe* your standard hillbilly is protecting. He's been squirreling away his family "honey" pot for years.

And in reality, the whole mountain dew lifestyle can get pretty complicated. You need to have a clean water source (a "branch"—as in, a river branch), something to cool the stuff down at the right time, something to heat it up at the right time, an infinite number of Mason jars, and some dope dense enough to play cupbearer to minimize the number of deaths. As most people know, once you put water, sugar, and yeast together, the yeast will eat the sugar and what you'll get is called "mash," and it will make you loopy—loopier the more you cook it down to pure alcohol. The finer points—where the sugar comes from (sloes, potatoes, bran, kudzu), where and how you cook it down, how lazy you are about washing things before and after you distill—that's handed down by word of mouth from each backwoods father to his son.

It's not illegal to know this information. If we weren't so protected by cleanliness and take-out Chinese, it would take less time to stumble on the recipe for hooch than it would for vulcanized rubber, in the average kitchen. It's a domestic chore like making jam or canning tomatoes. In Europe what we call moonshining is just The Homemade. Farmers have placed their jars of French calvados, Italian grappa, Spanish orujo, Swedish vodka, and Dutch ginebra on the table before me and it would have been a personal insult not to take a nip. It's also sensible to use every part of the grapevine, not to waste. There are people wicked-sober in Africa.

Sometimes the battle seems a lot of playacting, I think, another version of cops and robbers. That Whiskey Rebellion was a setup by Alexander Hamilton to force a battle between Federalists and the fiercely individual states, and had more to do with taxation than it did whiskey. As with any realm in which authority is at stake, the players, criminals, and police are so very close together the only thing that separates them is the thin blue line of the law and where you happen to be standing, at the moment, in relation to it.

.&.

I have never actually seen a moonshine still before, which begs the question, how can you write about something you don't know? But the whole bootleg operation exists mostly in our collective imagination. We would rather have a vision of a still in our dreamy heads, a jewel, gleaming in the woods. I see it there, well constructed and well designed, or better, distinguished, an old seasoned copper kettle generations old. The reality is always messier. Plastic and extra tubing littering the ground, the stink of sour mash, rats—and guns, always guns to shoot trespassers, and just to shoot off when you're blind drunk. Oh, and dogs. Howlin' flabby-skinned, varmint-chasin' smellhounds to bark loud when the guns are shot off.

And I take it back, grudgingly. As a boy, I did see a still, but it was in a buddy's garage, and it was constructed from a tube running from a mop bucket, through a plastic milk jug, to a beat-up, burnt-orange Crock-Pot procured at my own parents' garage sale. That was not romantic. It was humiliating.

To me moonshining is an inoffensive industry as harmonious with the natural order as a beehive or a tap in a tree capturing nature's spendthrift sap, just one small extra sensible step to mother nature: usefulness. Here we find our utilitarian aims working with nature, not against it.

Until, that is, you actually think about it. I'm as guilty as anybody of indulging in the myth of the American Pastoral. I am like one of those noble-born, lily-livered poets two hundred years ago who sat under a tree and wrote gushy odes to the inner peace and happiness of the peasants out laboring in the fields. If I only watch, then I won't get my hands dirty. The way men watch—it's a way of remaining pure.

I have never seen a non-Crock-Pot moonshine still, but in the open woodland that separated my high school and the neighborhood where I grew up, evidence of all manner of human intervention could be found. It was almost Jungian as a holding place, this small patch of what I perceived as wilderness, a place where I stumbled on a dead Dalmatian that had a hole in its side—from a fight? From a bullet wound?—near the swamp; a bag of porno magazines resting against a tall pine, nearly imperceptible tree forts and ground forts built by bad high school kids; piles of blankets and spent condoms that gave evidence of illicit sex.

And then there was the day I was walking in the black acidic low muck and found six stately rows of tomato plants lovingly tended, a spade, and a half-used plastic bag of fertilizer neatly stacked, accessed through a wall of briars so thick that only the most adventurous loner boy would dare scratch himself up getting through it. But where were the tomatoes? And why did the stalks of the tomato plants splay in that maple-leaf-like way? And did I smell oregano? Gasp: marijuana. My blood ran cold. This forest primeval had suddenly become the potential site of a drug-related murder (mine), or a frame job (also mine) that would send me straight to juvie. I remember running for it, getting even more scratched up by racing through the briar patch. I think I experienced a first run-in with irony when I got grounded that day for getting my shoes all mucky.

It was only a matter of course that the service project I mapped out, instrumental in earning me the rank of Eagle Scout, was to direct my entire troop into that open space with garbage bags, shovels, and rakes to clean up nature. And it shouldn't be a surprise that it took a very unsexy *team* to do the good deed.

The woods were the place where I found the proof of all the things that I knew people did, in theory, in the flesh. That these aberrations were first introduced to me in the setting of nature did some funky mojo on my sense of what my role in nature truly is. Nature is wild, without order. If a man can handle that chaos, he can handle anything, right? Well, maybe not. Nature's chaos frees a man from all those rules and judgments that burden him when he has to be a team player in our unsexy civilization.

Outside the woods there are faceless corporations selling you products you don't want, stone-faced bill collectors sending you invoices for the products you didn't want, edifaced IRS auditors asking you to pay taxes on the products you didn't want. Preachers, lawyers, bureaucrats, goddamn commies. In the Reagan-era blockbuster movie *Red Dawn*, scary Soviets took over America the Beautiful by first landing in a schoolyard and killing the history teacher. But wouldn't real All-Americans be rather pleased to see the history teacher killed? Hegel once explained that modern man lived in history, not nature. The Old Countries embrace that notion, especially Russian commies, who were quite damaged by the march of history. American he-men, however (and here I speak of us *all* as American he-men), basically hate that idea. History is ugly and dirty, nature is pretty and pure. Real guys like to tromp out into the woods to be pure, and they can pretend that all those porn mags, condoms, blankets, cool forts, hemp crops, and moonshine stills just *appeared* there, just sprang from the fertile earth, floated downriver from that pure source.

The Europeans are buried under their burden of history and seem to have completely eschewed nature (whether we're talking about French people chain smoking or decrepit, leaky Russian nuclear power plants or the endless marble and concrete of the new Berlin governmental buildings); the idea of anything being done in harmony with nature seems incongruous there. We Americans are morally appalled.

For we love our lawns. We love our landscape paintings unpeopled (it strikes me while touring American art museums that most of them were, until the occasional person grudgingly appeared in them after the messy shame of the Civil War, our first besmirchment of God's Country), baby animals, and infants, free of experience and worldly knowledge. We go down to the river, nature's bosom, the soul's own clean branch, to be baptized, washed of our sin. And when we imagine a moonshiner's operation, we prefer to see it as a gleaming apparition, an oasis in the forest—never in a cinder block room or in a city. Or in a freakin' Crock-Pot in my buddy's garage. We see it draped with camouflage or canopied by trees to make it even more a part of nature. Walk softly, hillbilly friend. There is a tentative but real connection between rum-running and health food, between grain alcohol and amber waves of grain—dude, try some— it's totally organic.

Even the big beer companies with silos full of fermenting hops want us to think they're a Cousin George operation, making us the pure unbesmirched stuff bare-handed. The water for the beer comes from real mountain springs—you know, the "Bud Branch"—some old guy is measuring the hops with a measuring spoon swiped from his wife's kitchen, and tiny Italian ladies are squashing the grapes under their dainty virgin toes. If there must truly be an intermediary, it is better that it's just one small person and not a host of too many cooks spoiling the broth.

*♪.*

Drinking the stuff, however, must be a social occasion. In my own personal vision of these Last Days, a time when we have nearly abandoned public life, when the town squares are for vagrants and when we protect ourselves from contact with strangers on the street by plugging into disc players and cell phones, when the vernacular architecture of new houses has traded in the wraparound porch for the two-car garage that opens only with the use of the remote, when Carl's Junior can sell burgers with the slogan "Don't Bother Me, I'm Eating," the last social occasion seems to be The Cocktail Party. Or, if you don't believe me, you can at least consider that drinking *alone* remains the ultimate antisocial act.

It may be heroic for one man to make the stuff, but it's not heroic to drink it alone. Even the antisocials know only losers enter a bar solo. Saturday night's all right for fighting: the manly art of tossing them back. But you have to have a witness—"bro, did you see Markansaw chug that whole pitcher of PBR? He is a gutbustin' *monster*."

Markansaw's manly poet friend wisely explained the challenge of heavy drinking after the age of thirty-five: you have to do it every day, or it doesn't stick. Markansaw's Cousin George warned us that something often happened when you drank his home brew: people tended to lose their shoes. I have been trying to get rid of a beat-up pair of Keds for a couple of years, so I invited the usual suspects over for a barbecue, and my corn-fed Iowan boy Grant made "Moo Burgers" to soak up the liquor. Moo Burgers are another kind of family tradition passed down from Grant's Carolina mother, requiring a kosher nightmare of hamburger, sour cream, Worcestershire sauce, and Kellogg's Frosted Flakes (accept no substitutes), grilled. I would give you the exact measurements but that would be about as illegal as giving you the instructions on how to build a still.

I, like Markansaw, come from a family of happy drinkers. With us there has never been a case of belligerent fighting after tossing back a few. We get sloppy and start telling boob jokes and blab things we ought not to blab (my mother, at my youngest brother's wedding reception, grabbed my arm and thanked me for not marrying that Leslie girl I dated in high school), but nobody drives, unless you count golf carts, and nobody gets hurt, unless you count my dog when she has been fed three Moo Burgers under the table by shoeless drunks. When friends tell me about the horrible way in which family members destroyed their lives and others' because of alcoholism, I thank my stars that alcohol has destroyed very little in my life. My experience with liquor, in fact, has been nearly profound when not merely silly—in vino veritas. Suddenly I understand Hart Crane's poetry, Scriabin's music, and Odilon Redon's paintings.

Grant, The Moo Burgermeister, had one of those bad-drinking families. So he only sips now and then. His Midwestern Lutheranism prohibits him from swearing much (unless you call "dangnabbit" and "h-e-double-toothpicks" swearing), and his idea of a naughty thing to do in the woods is to "pee wherever I wanted to." His drinking experiences are few, so a draw on the Mason jar is all he needed for the night.

After our first sips from Cousin George's jar, we shared a round-robin of fond memories of alcohol consumption—Jill remembered how she used to make whiskey sours using the very classy Ancient Age brand for her grandmother when she was a little girl, not quite knowing what she was doing. (Her grandmother would hold out her sweaty glass while never missing a beat with her rocking chair and say, "Jill, be a sweetie and getcher grammaw another lemonade.") Owen and Markansaw and I reminisced about all those times we drank too much, and boasted about the subsequent hurling. Markansaw said that the code word for moonshine, at least in his neck of the woods, is "honey." This is a standard term apparently, and many moonshiners, in that do-it-yourself spirit, actually do raise bees and jar honey. I don't think it's really a front—would it be worth it to go through all that work and multiple stings if they didn't really want to manufacture honey? I think they actually carry on the two operations with equal zeal.

Drinking should be a team sport, not a lone gunman thing. Whether alcohol is a cause or effect of our behavior—whether the alcohol makes us act out of character or in fact inflates our already innate character—it magnifies or crystallizes us, and separates us, as we were in that high school culture of yore, into the socials and the loners.

What surprised us was how smooth the stuff was. You always see guys on *Hee-Haw* taking a draw on a triple-X jug and sputtering, cartoon steam coming out of their ears, near death: "dat's *gid*." But moonshine is different from white lightning. White lightning is that ethanol you get once you do just the basic yeast process and cook it down to everclear. Moonshine has pretensions to pedigree, and may even be aged in fine oak barrels. Liquor takes on the flavor of the fruit from which it has been fermented, but also the container in which the distillation occurs. I wonder whether the moonshine in my buddy's garage Crock-Pot took on the tang of my mom's spaghetti sauce? We actually had a vertical tasting from two different jars Markansaw brought from two years. The darker one was mellow, aged in oak. We were impressed. Then we lost our shoes.

I've got my own forced-innocent ideas imposed on moonshine, besides my recurring image of a shiny corrugated tank on stilts glowing like a beacon under a full moon, some kind of shelter from the clements, bodily comfort. I want moonshine to fit into my idea of living efficiently and simply with nature, and I want to believe that this is the way for poor folk to enjoy what I can go to the grocery store and get. I want it to be one of those generational things too, like quilting, just like they say. According to the Bureau of Alcohol, Tobacco and Firearms, even though moonshining is considered a dying art like churning your own butter, there may be more illegal production today than there was thirty years ago. And that same bureau spends most of its energy waging wars on drugs and keeping tabs on the guns, so Billy Bob's woodpile is pretty far down their list. They ought to call it the BTFA, not the BATF. Still, they seized 538 stills in a small portion of Virginia in the last fifteen years. That's a lot of honey. And that amount makes me think harder about what the culture, at large, wants.

I'm terrible at that. I am puzzled by pop music and fashion trends. Why, I wonder, would anybody *want* that? And I never know when everybody wants something until it has been mediated. That is, if comedy troops make fun of or imitate an actor or singer, I understand that this mocked person must be a celebrity. You've made it, to me, if you appear as a clue in the *New York Times* crossword puzzle. I don't know what is considered a status symbol until I see a wrecked version of it (a nonfunctioning cell phone, a DKNY T-shirt) in the shopping cart of a homeless person. I don't know what's fashionable until it has been knocked off. Good old Jill was walking down the street with me and we were listening to two Filipino women chatting in that jabbery run-on Tagalog until one of them stopped dead in her tracks and her sentence, right in front of a card table set up on the sidewalk covered with counterfeit designer purses. She gasped, "Ohhhh, Kate Spade!" Now I know who Kate Spade is. Since imitation is the highest form of flattery, the cheap version of alcohol, whether it's schnapps or bourbon or wine, reveals to me just how much people like their sippin' liquor.

What's the average Joe to do? There are so many luxuries in our rich nation and we need somebody to sort them all out. We need a mediator. Reviewers and critics and dim-witted cupbearers. Except they're all trying to sell something. That leaves many of us with a desire to run up into the mountains to grow our own crops, start our own religion, make our own honey, and set up a still. And git the hell off my property, you damn revenuer man, or I'll fill yer hide with buckshot!

That's one of the reasons I like do-it-yourself projects, illegal or no. In an age of press releases and manufactured desire, a clear sign that something is truly desired in the deepest nether reaches of the heart would be exhibited by the fact that the object of desire was made by hand: necessity is the mother of invention.

Men go into the woods for all sorts of crafty reasons, but ironically, they go there primarily to find innocence again—an escape from history. Too bad they drag their baggage full of history with them, and the woods become the place where innocence ends. I recall that soon after I was grounded for muddying my shoes while discovering weed growing in the weeds, the whole secret guilty world was revealed to me. I began to have what teenaged girls call a "personal life," I suppose—a secret life. The hidden woodsy world is where real desires are fulfilled in a homemade fashion.

My initial discovery of the secret world of gay men, for instance, felt just like that sinking realization I experienced when I stumbled on the pot plants. The sinking feeling had exhibited itself in other instances too, like the time I read the story of Oedipus solving the riddle of the Sphinx in a children's book, a version that ended abruptly with him becoming king of Thebes and living happily ever after.

Why do we subject children to this kind of censorship? It's only a matter of time before we find out Oedipus killed his father and married his mother and plucked out his eyes. And then we feel tricked, we sense that certain facts, certain stories, heretofore hidden in the woods, are dirty and shameful. Disney's cleaned-up versions of fairy tales, in which Cinderella's wicked stepsisters did not cut off their own toes to fit into the glass slipper or in which the little mermaid does not feel stinging cuts on her feet when she reveals her identity, create the same sort of filthy feeling. Disney, like all amnesiac instances of contrived innocence, makes me feel dirty—because I am not innocent.

In the same way, home brewing and underage drinking of home brewing is not nearly the problem in other countries that it is in our nation hell-bent on keeping us pure. If there is nothing that makes you want to make moonshine more than the establishment of laws forbidding the making of moonshine, there is nothing that makes you less enthusiastic about drinking than having full permission to do so.

I knew that there was guilt by association, and it only makes sense that gay men often connect while wandering in wooded parks and secluded rest areas—in nature, as we were meant to be, searching for a do-it-yourself still to make whatever truly is our do-it-yourself desire.

But who's gonna help you build your still, tote your

bushel, bear your cup? Maybe playing on a team isn't as unsexy as all that. I'm thinking about baseball again. When we got spontaneous erections as boys, older boys who already knew personally the heartbreak of doing math problems on the classroom chalkboard with a woody advised us to think of something really unsexy. Baseball, for example. Baseball is the opposite of sex. It's a team sport. But that trick doesn't work for everybody. I ask you: what about former Giants catcher Bobby Estalella? Teams can be sexy. Especially when they get the job done.

Making moonshine is a committee procedure, but the submission to compromise, creating the necessary bureaucracy of bootlegging, is its own reward, celebrated during the necessary bureaucracy of drinking in celebration. It took me twenty years to stop wrinkling my nose at the smell of team spirit, and I'm thrilled that at such a point in an adult life, a guy can discover new enthusiasms. Grant has been taking me to a lot of baseball games lately. I don't exactly get spontaneous erections anymore, but I sure get excited. Grant says I swear too much, but usually I'm swearing at the prima donnas who aren't good team players.

There's a familiar folk song called "The Big Rock Candy Mountain." As a boy, I mistook it for just another lullaby like "Winken, Blinken, and Nod" or "The Sugarplum Tree"; geewhiz, a mountain made of candy, where bluebirds sing near lemonade springs, and there's the buzz of bees around the peppermint trees, and you never had to wash your face or change your socks—an innocent child's fondest desire. I didn't know it was secretly as dark and knowing as the stepsisters' fates, or Oedipus's destiny, or the dark draw of the virgin forest. It wasn't until I was a grown-up, and knew what a still was, and knew what the spent condoms meant, and recognized the significant looks of men wandering the perimeters of wooded parks, that I heard the true, unchanged version of that old folk song.

In the real Big Rock Candy Mountain, true, you never change your socks, but there's little streams of alkyhol that come trickling down the rocks—not lemonade. The cops have wooden legs, the hens lay soft-boiled eggs, they hung the jerk who invented work, and there's the buzz of bees— around the cigarette trees, not peppermint trees. For you see, the Big Rock Candy Mountain is not the promised land of innocent children, but of liquor-loving hobos. I'd go there now, but I seem to have misplaced my shoes somewhere.

# 15

# THE OLD MAN AND THE SPA

OF COURSE, I'M GOING TO DIE ANYWAY. THIS melodramatic thought comes to me most often in moments of conciliatory luxury. I thought it as I lowered myself into a massive marble tub full of spa water, the most healthful water, reportedly, to be found in any health spa in the world.

"All these essential vitamins and minerals," I said to my attendant, "I feel like presweetened cereal." I said it just to be polite, since this guy probably didn't speak a word of English.

The attendant was at least seventy and had a shock of perfectly white wavy hair, all combed neatly upward—like the symbol for the heater on a car dashboard, or like smoke pouring out of a barbecue vent. His eyebrows, however, were two dark patches, the hair that grew in birthmarks; carpet samples. He was lame and I was sure he had been for life.

Probably, I thought further, the old guy hadn't ventured far beyond the walls of this sanitarium, sent here in sickly childhood by a doctor and staying, depending so much on the healing waters that he just started working there one day and then, poof!, he was seventy.

I had composed a whole history for the attendant while waiting with a traveling companion in one of a long line of sleek cushioned reclining chairs fixed into the tile floor (the waiting hall was almost empty except for a snoozing Germanic-looking man with—good God!—a *goiter*). I'd heard the limping old guy approach and recede into the room he was preparing for me, the left leg half the size of his normal leg, which echo-squeaked in the sanitarium like gym shoes on a basketball court.

"Or brandy," the attendant said now, without a smidgen of accent, folding a fat thirsty towel over the chair. I was going to say a surprised thing like, "Wow, you speak English," or "Wow, you made a joke," but something further distracted me.

"I'm green!" I said, looking at my body submerged in the healthy steamy soup of whatever ran down five different copper pipes into the tub.

"Sulfur," agreed the attendant, "and iron. Now I have to go prepare the other room for your friend," he said, seeing me settled.

"Come back if you get bored," I splashed. The attendant smiled. Oh God, would he want a tip? What were the gratuity policies in the Azores? Tipping is the worst aspect of travel.

When the door clicked shut I assessed the room—a cube tiled white from floor to ceiling, trimmed bright yellow. The single wooden chair with my towel, a small pointless changing stall where all my clothes hung on a single hook, a big glazed window, a toilet with a roll of strikingly pink toilet paper.

I had flushed the toilet before disrobing, as a part of an ongoing experiment I'd been conducting here and throughout the world, and at this point, I feared that Portuguese toilets were designed only to rinse the doodies, not get rid of them. In the hotels I'd stayed in on the emerald islands of Terceira, Flores, and now São Miguel, I'd been given bathrooms with that party-guest-nightmare toilet problem. Here

at the health-minded spa (in Portuguese, *termas*) Terra
Nostra however, where cleanliness was paramount and state
run, the toilet neither rinsed nor flushed, but seemed to
eradicate waste into another dimension, and made way too
much noise in the process.

From the tub across the too-big room, the toilet seemed
to be shrinking and lonely, but the paper was still fifi-pink.

I leaned my head against the stone. By now, my travel
partner Michael was settled into his own tub. Michael was a
good travel planner, but a leader with no followers. He kept
me moving along when I might have stayed in the garden all
day rather than walk into town or take a look at a local bar.

Michael was also what the *San Francisco Chronicle* back
home called, in a business section story about the success of
the cable Weather Channel, a target market known as "The
Weather Involved." And the Azores is the source of a lot of
weather. Europeans hate to hear meteorological news from
the Azores—it means a storm is coming.

Rain beat on the roof of the Furnas Sanitarium with the
violence of invading armies, or that toilet over there. The day
after this long soak, I would be just as transfixed as Michael
when the television news showed image after image of flood
damage: overflowing rivers, chocolate waterfalls into the
Atlantic, a little dog floating cutely around a deluged living
room on a sofa cushion. Touring around for the rest of this trip,
I would feel like an insurance adjuster rather than a tourist. But
I'd also feel a secret dark privilege to have seen this disaster.

I posed for myself like I'd just discovered specific gravity,
one finger in the air. The rain drummed so loudly I didn't
hear the attendant return. I was caught in my pose and
scrambled for an excuse. "I was doing my imitation of
Archimedes. Eureka! You know."

The attendant smiled. "When my son comes here to visit, he likes to do the great bathtub tragedies. It's a routine he does. First he wraps his head in a towel and does Jean-Paul Marat. Then he lies back with a little wad of toilet paper like posies, and he's Ophelia. Then he sits with pots of coffee and paper and scratches himself like Balzac with his galleys and skin conditions."

I took it all in.

"You thought I was a stupid Azorean peasant, didn't you?" said the man.

I would not have said stupid. I sank lower in the water. I had a pain in my neck from the too-flat posture-beneficial pillows at the hotel.

"You know that if you're sick, there are special treatments and a free doctor consultation," he said, thump-squeaking over to the chair and taking a load off.

"I'm not sick, though," I said, trying to keep defensiveness out of my voice. "I come for the spa. I come to a health resort to keep healthy. Tonight we're going to lower a chicken into one of your boiling hot craters and cook it and eat it with a fizzy bottle of green wine. And then tomorrow morning we're going to hike along the edge of a volcano."

"So you're liking the Azores."

Was I? I'd been blowing all my travel on the great spas of Europe in the last few years: sunflowered Montepulciano, geriatric Orion in the Catalan hinterland, spas en Spa, Baden am Baden-Baden, baths in Bath. The vague boredom of taking the waters in those towns was mitigated by history, architecture, ponderous churches, and cafés. The Azores were Michael's idea. Here in Furnas, what was there? A wide ferruginous orange-brown pool, hydrangeas that strangled all other form of plant life, comical arts and crafts like flowers made out of fish scales, uninteresting ceramics, and ugh, scrimshaw peace signs and Playboy bunny heads.

Rain beat down even harder. Distracted by the torrent, I had to ask loudly, "Do you always get rain like this?"

The man shook his head. "Never so early. December once or twice, but by then they're ready. The birds' nests are cleaned out of the roof tiles so they can drain. But never in September. This will be some trouble."

I imagined this man as a boy, cleaning tiles on his house with a stick. "You've lived here all your life?"

"Hell no. Moved to New Bedford when I was nine and lived there until I was sixty-five. The wife wanted peace and quiet." That explained his excellent English. He'd been speaking it almost twice as long as I had been alive. "I wanted the water. Got to be close to the water."

"It's good for your leg," I pointed at the shrunken limb, draped with his white sanitary smock.

"For fishing!" The man seemed offended. It wasn't supposed to be obvious, obviously. "For the soul!"

"Oh, for the soul, the soul. How come everybody but me knows so much about the soul? What's good for it, what's bad for it."

"You're a gay, aren't you?" said the man. It was retaliation; I reveal his lameness, he reveals my sexuality.

"Yes, a gay." I liked the "a." It made me feel like an item.

"My son is one in Boston." He leaned forward. I had nothing to say to that, so the man said, "I'm hoping he doesn't die. He's older than you." He got up to do a squeaky circle around the chair like a dog on a tether. "He has the virus, but he hasn't been sick. Now he's got the new medicines."

"That's nice," I sank into the enriched water until only my head stuck out. I was feeling very much found out.

"And I pray for him every day to the Espiritu Santu." This, he said in Portuguese, so that "Espiritu" sounded vaguely obscene, "Shpurtoo."

Espiritu Santu, the Holy Spirit: the Azores find their greatest strength and patron in that most oblique of all religious entities, invisible, characterless. It was supposed to be the mysterious, most imaginative part of the Trinity— Father, Son, Blankety-Blank—and therefore without physical attributes. But ever since the Church came up with the concept way back when, everybody has tried to give the spirit a body anyway, form, substance. The most common renditions are of a dove, or a crown.

.ʎ.

Near our hotel there was a repair shop for religious figurines. Icons and statues were being repaired, touched up, and remolded by a skillful old man: a broken Virgin, an old Santiago in need of a paint job; a fat baroque cherub with a busted butt cheek. The faithless can only be jealous of those with faith. I know I am. There in the corner, is Saint Roche's dog, with a loaf of bread in his mouth, waiting to be reunited with his master.

Saint Roche, who probably lived in the late fourteenth century, is the patron saint of invalids and plague victims. In paintings and statues, he is always depicted as a pilgrim, with a staff and a hat with the symbol of keys on it. He is always shown lifting his own skirts and revealing a wound on his inner thigh, and there is a little dog at his feet with a loaf of bread in his mouth.

Supposedly Saint Roche was on his way to Rome and found all of Italy plague-stricken. He stopped his journey in order to help the sick in the numerous cities. He is attributed with the miracle of curing hundreds of plague victims simply by making the sign of the cross over them. Eventually he was infected himself (hence, the wound) and not wanting to infect others, he went out into the woods to die.

But God sent him a little dog, his mouth full of daily bread, to look after him. When he regained his health, Roche went on to cure more people as well as their cattle. He died in prison but when they examined his body, they found a cross-shaped birthmark, proving he was the long-lost son of the governor who once ruled the town.

Saint Roche's story satisfies for a handful of reasons. He was a pilgrim. His chapels are everywhere along the road to Santiago. He had a pet. And he is the patron saint of plague victims.

On a more profane note, that wound on his inner thigh has inspired artists through the centuries to show their skill at depicting the male physique. Others have made it erotic, forcing Roche to lift his clothes higher and higher until some of the more rococo versions offer what is ostensibly a wide-open beaver shot—the wound is vaginal, and Roche appears half-man, half-woman.

Religion, like machismo, like healthy family relations, is a thing that many gay men have mostly learned to do without. For some reason, I have been made to feel more comfortable around men with hunting rifles, Portuguese longshoremen and fishermen, or sitting in my local African-American Catholic church, with full gospel choir, than I have in gay bars or discos. Gay men have given me far more grief about going to church than priests have.

Three days after the Azorean baths, I would be in the city of Ponta Delgada unsuccessfully trying to use a credit card to get escudos out of an ATM administered by the

Banco Espiritu Santu. Even the money was invested in the Holy Spirit.

When the machine did not give, I turned around and had an immediate view of the ocean. A strange light eked through the clouds onto the surface, somehow miniaturizing that vast body of water, and it looked to me like the Red Sea in Cecil B. DeMille's *The Ten Commandments*, which I had heard was done with gelatin. Just then, the church bells of São Pedro rang.

"It's Sunday," Michael said. "Maybe the bank won't give us money on Sunday."

I checked my watch. It was an odd hour to ring bells, 11:37 A.M. The song of the bells sounded urgent and complex and Chinese, with point and counterpoint. I decided that the tune was set on a mechanical roll many years ago, for a certain set of tuned bells, and as one or two at a time over time were replaced because of wear and tear or earthquakes or whatever, the tones of the bells no longer matched each other. Who would ever know the lost tune made foreign? I want to use the words "harsh" and "sour" to describe it, but that's unfair; it pleased me. "They're consecrating the host," I realized.

.&.

At the sauna, I listened to the attendant talk about praying to the Holy Spirit. "It can't hurt, can it?" he shrugged. "You're a Catholic."

I wondered whether the guy read tea leaves too. "Now how would you know that?"

"Because it bothers you when I talk about praying to the Holy Spirit. If you were Protestant or Jewish, you'd be amused."

"I don't even know what the Holy Spirit is," I sat up again. When I got too warm in the water I had to stick a leg out like a chimney to release the heat. "Everybody is telling me about invisible things happening to me. Why should I believe it? I have the virus, yes, but I've never been sick, just like your son. Why should I believe I have it? And those new medicines that are helping your son? The doctor says they're saving me, but why should I believe her?"

Two years before, I had been sitting in the murky steam of the YMCA sauna, which was nearly empty except for a hunky Latino guy, who began to grasp my thigh and then slipped his other hand between my legs. I reciprocated. I had not planned it, planning was for people who believed in the future; this was something to take advantage of. I ran a hand down the guy's shocking smoothness, and just then a familiar hulking man stormed in through the steam. He'd been fast enough to catch me red-handed, and sat scowling across from me, the boiling sauna machine between us like a magic cauldron. The Latino guy had fled to the locker room, but I was rooted to the spot. The scowling man, heavily muscled with long brown hair, said to me, "You shouldn't do that. It's bad for your soul."

That reproach chaffed over the years, more than any anti-gay slur. I'd seen this guy many times before—he was a frequent punching-bag user, a boxer. He cultivated some kind of ascetic aura by being silent, solitary. Was boxing better for the soul? Punching somebody in the head, was it more purifying than running a searching hand over a body in mutual pleasure?

"It's a mystery," said the lame man. "Fate, my wife calls it."

"I'm just supposed to accept it, like you must accept your son being born gay, or having a lame leg."

The attendant laughed. He seemed to rally now and then from a tired decrepitude; certain things I said wound him up like a toy. "I wasn't lame from birth! I was a longshoreman for forty years, hauling heavy things until one day a block and tackle swung by and crushed my leg." He rolled up his pant leg for me to see: it was prosthetic, a big piece of plastic.

We could hear Michael down the hall, singing Gilbert and Sullivan at the top of his lungs. *"What never? No never! What never? Well, hardly ever! He's hardly-yever sick! At! Sea!"*

"Will that be bothering the other guests?" I asked.

"There are no other guests, you're it. It's the off-season." The Azores had seemed curiously abandoned to me, well-paved roads and empty grand hotels and expansive airports to handle just two or three flights a day. Empty shops with hopeful signs for nonexistent tourists: "We Perform the Lay Away." Towns without restaurants, nor cafés, listless cabbies at the taxi stands. Cows on the roadway. The old attendant shrugged. "I know you will find it hard to believe, but I was handsome once and my wife was considered very plain."

"What was the attraction?"

"She played hard-to-get. She could dance and swear and cook. Do you know our fish in the Azores, the one called espada? It's black and ugly with a grimace full of teeth and pop eyes, big ones so they can see in the dark at the bottom of the ocean. It's the most delicious fish you ever ate, grilled, baked, boiled with a banana in a caldera."

"And you fell in love with your wife because she cooks great espada."

"No, my wife *looks* like an espada. But I love her. She's always been mysterious, like she's still got a few secrets from me."

"Like the Holy Spirit."

♪.

The day before, we had returned to our luxurious old-money Hotel de São Pedro and found the turndown service had left us not chocolates on the bedside table, but a little card. The Azores, colonized by fishermen and navigators and farmers, were also Weather Involved. The card read: "Dear Guest, we wish you a very good night. Here is the weather forecast for tomorrow. May it help you to enjoy another day in S. Miguel." And below that, four symbols: a sun, clouds, an umbrella, and a thermometer. The clouds were checked, and the thermometer was filled up to the 25-degree centigrade mark.

"How will this help us enjoy São Miguel?" I asked Michael, who loved this little four-star touch.

"If it rains, we'll know. We can plan around it."

But it did rain the next day. You can't forecast weather where weather begins.

♪.

"What if you discover your wife's little secret, and it turns out to be something lame, like a birthmark on the top of her head, or a Madeiran in her lineage?"

"My wife is Jewish. I met her in the restaurant where she cooked in New Bedford."

"Jewish? And she doesn't mind being here with all these Catholics? She doesn't mind you praying to the Holy Spirit for the life of your sick gay son?"

"She doesn't know he's a gay, or sick."

This might have been irritating, all these false appraisals (I considered myself able to imagine character quickly) I had made. If there had been a third person in the room, like the boxing man who knew so much about the soul, I might have been furious. But alone with the mercurial attendant, the proposing and disposing had a merry nasty quality to it, Bugs Bunny and Daffy Duck ripping notice off of notice from the tree: "Duck Season! Wabbit Season! Duck Season! Wabbit Season!" until it came down to some as yet unknown punch line: Elmer Season?

"Why are you staring at me?" he asked.

"You're furious with me," I sat up, for the truth of it came to me as it came out of my mouth. "And you're furious at your son. You can't believe we did what we did to endanger our lives and that we weren't good enough to ourselves—to our souls—to save us from doom."

"That's crazy," he said, kneading a place on his thigh where, perhaps, his artificial limb connected with his flesh.

"Can I tell you something? All that 'ruining my health'?—It was fun. Every minute of it was a blast. I'll bet your son agrees, even if he doesn't tell you. When you smoke cigarettes, when you toss back a drink, it's great. The rest of the time, you just sit around paying the consequences and you think, how is it that the most terrible thing in my life is also the most wonderful thing in my life?"

The man crossed his arms. I could easily imagine him as a powerful foreman in the glory days of the unions on the docks, ordering stevedores around, cussing up a storm. To be so powerful in the body once, and then to have a leg shattered. To think you knew it all, how life worked, and then your kid is queer and sick. Wherein resides the soul? In the body or in the brain? What does it look like, and what does it any good? Good acts? Good thoughts?

"Let me ask you something," I said. The water had completely relaxed me. After this visit, I would never see this man again. I flourish in anonymous encounters. Strange men in saunas, priests behind confessionals, fellow pilgrims stopping on the same night in the same inn. "Do you think that if you sit here with me, it's good for you? For your soul?"

The attendant was agitated. He said, "Your friend is calling," and abruptly got up. Funny, I hadn't heard anybody. Suddenly I was alone. Alone, the room suddenly felt like a gas chamber to me, the pointlessly wide space had a killing-room feel to it, easy to hose down afterward.

As we moved through these islands, I felt the ghostly sense that the whole place was abandoned. There were more buildings than needed and all the population was heading away. The ones who stayed had an edge of island fever, exhibited in the mad way they drove cars down narrow alleys, like furious hornets mudded into their own nests.

But this was an island vacation. After the tour of the Azores, we moved on to another Portuguese possession, the island of Madeira. There, in a tiny convent, I got my beloved statue of Saint Roche. The Convento Santa Clara has been for centuries the home of the kind of nuns that don't want to consort with people. "Cloistered," they call them. They attend mass behind a curtain as has been the custom for four centuries. Now the convent's occupants have been, as that old tragic guidebook phrase puts it, "reduced to a handful," and they are not so reclusive. One of them gives little tours of the convent. Two friends and I were on such a tour with one other person, an aged tourist from France. It has been my experience that whenever there is one French person in a group, the language we speak is French, and the nun giving us the tour, who must have been all of five feet tall, blathered on about *les chapelles*.

She was an energetic nun, scampering from chapelle to chapelle, revealing the gorgeous artwork and the history of the convent. The aged Frenchwoman could not keep up. Zipping up a flight of steep stairs, we noticed the old woman giving it up, unbeknownst to our guide. "But where did the Madame go?" she asked us in French.

"She couldn't make the stairs," we explained.

The nun shrugged and looked askance. "They aren't that steep." And with a "humph," she continued her tour. Still in French.

When we came near the end, we found one of the other sisters resting in a chair near a cabinet of figurines. She was palsied and lame, and had to stand up with the use of a sturdy crutch. Would we like to buy anything? She had hand-painted depictions of the Pietà, Saint Christopher, the Blessed Virgin Mary—and one of Saint Roche.

Heresy! Instead of the crossed keys on his hat, he had the cockleshell of a pilgrim to Santiago. I had to have him. She pulled him down for me. The paint job was terrible, her hands must've shook, the poor woman, trying to hold steady to paint on his beard, his little wound (a drip of red paint to show the messy gash). The little dog looked like it had been in a fistfight and got two black eyes, or was, as if by another miracle of Saint Roche, transforming himself into a raccoon or a drag queen.

The nun handed her crutch to our tour guide so she could make change and very nicely wrap the statue in paper with a ribbon. Her sister sister was getting impatient, and when the transaction was nearly completed, the little woman scurried on to show us two more chapels on the itinerary.

Just as we were about to turn the corner out of sight, I looked back to see the artist nun. She was hanging for dear life from the big cabinet full of figurines, shrieking for the return of her crutch, which was still in the hands of She Who Had Little Patience for the Infirm.

♪.

When the old Azorean attendant returned to my sauna room with the squeak-slide, squeak-slide, he seemed even more shrunken than before. He sat back down wearily; the smock had fallen away and now I could see deep into the front pocket of the man's pants. It was like the pocket of a schoolboy: I could see a pack of cigarettes, a ball of string, surrendered termas tickets, change, a penknife, keys, a wadded ball of aluminum foil. Maybe I just imagined some of it.

"Your friend is something of a ninny," he sighed. "He asked me to run more water for him because he's got a small leak in his tub, and when I turned on the water," he chuckled, "the heat from it made him make the funniest noise."

I knew the noise; I'd heard him when the hotel showers shifted heat abruptly. "He squeals like a guinea pig handled by too many kindergartners."

The man slapped his fake leg and laughed.

Then it was quiet again, except for a drop of water echoing against the tile.

The fish market in Ponta Delgada would remind me of this room when we encountered it a few days later. It was a vast room tiled and viewable from a gallery above. There were long stainless steel tables where squids were sorted by size and the hideous eel-like espada that the attendant spoke of hung off the edge like slick black belts waiting to be cut into steaks. A customer would select one and the tail of the beast would be stuck into its own spike-toothed mouth, the way a fox stole's head bit demurely on a paw over the shoulder of a dowager, before being handed over. They waited on row after row of tables that resembled the theater of an operating room, shiny silver tables best for the lidless unblinking eyes of fish.

I had watched the way the friends of fishermen would come up to the tables and greet these men, whose hands were completely gunked up by fish guts and blood. The clean friend would grab the fisherman by the forearm and shake it, to avoid getting gunked up too. I looked at Michael. This was the way it was between the two of us. He would always shake me at the forearm, to avoid getting gunked up.

"I am tired so quickly," sighed the man. All the fight was gone from him, his mind had wandered. He probably didn't remember what the two of us had talked about. The momentum of our discussion was lost. Did old age afford him forgetfulness now and then? Were there times when he did not remember that his own son was a time bomb ready to go off?

"Why don't you take a bath?" I suggested.

The man grinned, like the fish who miraculously understood and approved at the lakeside where Saint Anthony of Padua preached to them. "Because the attendant needs an attendant."

I stood up, dripping. "Undress."

"What?"

"Undress, I'm going to help you." I undid the man's smock by pulling the ties on the back, easy as shoestrings. I unbuckled the belt, removed the pants and shirt, not unlike a lover. "I don't know how to take off the leg."

The man had been silent until then. "Nobody knows how to take my leg off except me."

I watched him unstrap the apparatus. It suggested stays and snaps on underwear, a secret, a symbol. "You should show your wife how to unhook your leg," I grinned.

The man laughed. "Yes, I should."

The leg off, I couldn't believe how far up it went. Clairvoyant again, the attendant said, "And my hip was smithereens, too."

"Do you miss the shipyards?"

He seemed almost ready to cry. "I'd be there now if it weren't for this. Do you know how good hard work feels?"

I knew it was no reproach. I lifted the man to place him in the water. We were both naked.

"Don't you slip," he said.

I lowered him. I'd cared for Jeff and other sick friends long enough to know how to lift in the legs, not in the back. I sneaked a guilty peek at his stump, the way guys spy lined up at the urinal. Where his leg had been was a scarred gash. Saint Roche had nothing over this attendant saint.

The old man had his eyes shut and to me, his eyelids looked like the very center end of a roll of yellow crepe paper, where the crimps were more thickly compressed.

Down the hall, we heard Michael start up again: *"He's hardly ever sick at sea! Then give three cheers and one cheer more for the hardy captain of the Pinafore!"*

The man was submerged to the head. I sat satisfied on the wooden chair. It was quiet except for the singing down the hall, and the perfect roil of rain above.

"The ugly espada live in waters so deep," said the man

quietly, "scientists don't know anything about them. The fishermen drop lines down maybe a kilometer, and when they pull them up, the change in the pressure from coming up so far has already killed them, they die of the bends. And their eyes pop out. The fishermen put them back in so that they're more beautiful—ha, ha—to the buyers. Who knows how they live down there?"

"Maybe down there, they're beautiful," I said. I looked down at him. His wavy white hair had gone flat against his head and looked marcelled, as if the attendant was getting smaller, dissolving in the bath.

And this was the beginning of a long fierce time, about three days, in which it looked as if I were vanquishing the world, melted in rain, putting it on my terms for a change— I was emptied out, but so was everything.

"And as for the soul," said the man, who now ran his hands back and forth in front of himself, just below the surface of the green water, "whatever it is, it's more durable than anything around here, legs, hearts, heads. It's not the sickness that I am furious at. It's lack of love. What in the hell are you waiting for? And give me some more water."

I found the keys to the spigots in the pocket of boys' things, and I filled the big tub until it almost overflowed. I thought, I am not going to marry your son.

Outside, the rain was just as powerful, dissolving the whole world. There was no safe place, no way to protect the soul. But it was tough, tough enough to survive the deepest ocean depths. Its eyes were huge, to see in the dark.

It was not until three days later and after a delicious dinner of the ugly espadas smothered in a sauce of shrimps, that I thought perhaps an ex-longshoreman from New Bedford could possibly know more about the soul than me.

I can be dense when a major revelation is occurring. For grace is always unearned and unforeseen—unimaginable, wisdom from a one-legged fisherman, beautiful eyes in a poorly painted statue of Saint Roche, an ugly fish you don't know anything about that just tastes good.

# ACKNOWLEDGMENTS

Many people need to be thanked and blamed for this book. I could not have done it without Miriam Wolf, Larry Zapatka, Annalee Newitz, Paul Reidinger, Grant Burger, Chris Bouldrey, Jaime Bouldrey, Mark Bryles, Aaron May, Jill Olson, Owen Bly, David Kelley, Ralph Jassen, Rett Nelson, Elie Serfaty, Stephanie Rosenbaum, Glen David Gold, Dave Peattie, Michael Lowenthal, Martha McPartlin, Will Marion, Malcolm Margolin, Peter Revell, Adela Robles-Saèz, Lucy Jane Bledsoe, Jason K. Friedman, Sam Schad, Elizabeth Mosier, Jessica Neely, Charlie Ahern, Petra Wellemsen, Marta Maretich, Kevin Bentley, Bernard Shir-Cliff, Fiona Giles, Howard Junker, Victor Krummenacher, Bob Glück, Deborah Peifer, and that sweet inspiration, the band Red Meat. A shout-out to Porkchop, wherever you are.

These essays first appeared in slightly different forms in the following places: "Vallejo Killed the Rodeo Star," "Tammy and the Bachelor," "The Meat Men," "Lap Dance," "Smacked Down," "Oddfellows," "Blood, Sweat, and Tears," and "Clear Moonshine on an Evening of White Lightning" in the *San Francisco Bay Guardian*; "Monster" in *Chick for a Day*, edited by Fiona Giles; "Pilgrim's Regress" in *Zyzzyva* (reprinted in *Gay Travels*); portions of that essay were first printed in *Fourteen Hills*; portions of "Going to Extremes" (originally titled "What's Up Doc?") in *Flesh and the Word 4*, edited by Michael Lowenthal, and in *LA Weekly*. Portions of this book received a generous prize grant from the San Francisco Foundation's Joseph Henry Jackson Award for Nonfiction.